For years now, I have watche
of a kind that most of us wo
yet, in the midst of it, she is
a vibrant faith in the God she
meaning yet badly executed attempts of others to pray or exhort
her into health, she has dug down into the riches of Christ, the
eternal truths of the Bible and the persistent presence of her
God, and discovered the possibility of supernatural contentment.
If you live with chronic illness or disability, you will unearth real
treasures here. Everyone should read this and be encouraged
towards finding the contentment that Liz has learnt the hard
way and now reveals in her highly readable book.
Anne Coles, former leader, New Wine

This refreshingly honest book about holding on to faith, while
living with disabling ill health, names struggles that many share
but few express. In her charming and challenging voice, and
without clichés, Liz offers her own story, complete with the
raw darkness and light of experience. It's a gift worth receiving.
*Zoe Heming, Lichfield Diocese Enabling Church Adviser, vicar and
speaker*

Catching Contentment is beautifully written, its compelling
storytelling punctuated with profound biblical truth. But its real
beauty goes far deeper. In contrast to a culture consumed with
the pursuit of comfort and quick-fix solutions, it delves into the
reality of pain with moving first-hand experience. It is deeply
authentic, disarmingly vulnerable and teaches us all to hope,
trust and fight for contentment in every season of life. No
matter what your experience of suffering, this book is for you.
Phil Knox, Head of Mission to Young Adults, Evangelical Alliance

This is the best book I've read in the past five years! It's honest and
real and full of truth, but truth that builds up and encourages. It is
a journey into knowing that God doesn't always heal us physically
or change the painful circumstances in our lives. Rather, it affirms
that he will always 'come into the dust' of our sickness and pain
with us, bringing his transforming love and comfort.
Jennifer Rees Larcombe, author and speaker

This is the story of a faithful Christian who finds confidence in God in the midst of pain and distress. Liz Carter's quest for contentment, with its realistic and grounded awareness of how she and others suffer, is an effective antidote to the trivia we are often fed about God's protecting us from suffering because we are Christians. Her testimony – that you can find contentment in God even while living a life of pain – is both challenging and encouraging.
Roy McCloughry, National Disability Adviser, Church of England

Rather than promising a quick fix or cheap answers for shiny, happy people, Carter invites us on a compelling journey of fiercely pursuing God, even when we are wearied by disappointment and loss. As someone who also struggles with chronic illness, I found empathy, hope and spiritual sustenance. Biblically anchored, persuasively written theology, *Catching Contentment* is a must-read for any Christian who wrestles with a nagging desire for something more.
Tanya Marlow, writer at tanyamarlow.com and author of Those Who Wait *and* Coming Back to God When You Feel Empty

Liz has been incredibly open and honest in her beautifully written book. Not only does she weave in biblical wisdom but she also shares directly from the heart. I was so touched and inspired by the way she has fought for – and caught – contentment in the midst of incredibly difficult daily circumstances. I found *Catching Contentment* a wonderful addition to my own quiet time before God, and can heartily recommend it.
Claire Musters, speaker and author of Taking Off the Mask

Catching Contentment opened my eyes and introduced many new ideas and concepts that I'd never thought through before. The overriding message I'll take from it is that life truly is a journey of surrender to Christ as we move forward and let the past go. When we ask for and accept Christ's forgiveness, we can tap into his desires for our lives and seek to be content as we wait for his promises to be fulfilled. I loved the practical reflections, which draw us into the topic and help us to reflect on identity and contentment in a personal way.
Michelle Pannell, writer at Mummy from the Heart, the UK's leading Christian lifestyle and parenting blog

How we need this book at this time! In our consumerist world, lack can so easily erode faith and breed discontent. The 'ocean of meaningful words' inside Liz has spilled out in this wonderful book – a treasure trove created from plundering the Scriptures and the works of great Christian thinkers. With stories that inspire, prayers to nourish the soul and questions to search the mind and heart, *Catching Contentment* gives the reader an opportunity to form a biblical attitude and willingness to understand and endure suffering. It is a passionate reminder, from someone who lives each day with challenges and limitations, that as we fix our eyes on Jesus and pursue him wholeheartedly, a profound shift will happen, and we will experience true freedom and contentment. This book will excite you afresh about giving your all to pursuing Jesus wholeheartedly, counting everything else as nothing for the prize of gaining him.
Nadine Parkinson, Tearfund's New Wine Relationship Manager and developer of Tearfund/New Wine Change a Nation initiative

Two of the biggest questions in our culture are 'Where can I find contentment?' and 'How could a loving God allow suffering?' In this profound book, Liz Carter tackles both questions head on, and discovers that reflection on the second holds the keys to answering the first.

This moving and thoughtful study originated in the reality of Liz's own struggle with lifelong illness – always honest but never self-indulgent. But it is also rooted in meditating on key passages of Scripture as she wrestles with the challenges of her experience. Lastly, it is also grounded in the experience and thinking of other Christians who have struggled with similar questions in the face of personal suffering.

Full of profound observations, *Catching Contentment* will be an important resource for those living with illness and pain, those who minister with and to them, and those who need to think these things through – which covers all of us! This book unmasks the lie that fulness of life means always getting what we want, and holds out the hope of finding true contentment in God.
The Revd Dr Ian Paul, theologian, author and speaker

We live in an age of profound dissatisfaction with everything: health, relationships, self-image, lifestyles, finances – the list is endless. But here is a book that courageously digs deeply to help us find lasting contentment. This is not a work of platitudes or theories; Liz Carter lives with a long-term painful and limiting condition, and writes out of the disappointment, suffering and darkness that she has experienced. She bravely confronts the issues that she and others grapple with, digging out wells of truth to live by. Contentment is not a passive thing: it is a conscious choice, based on God's truth embraced and applied. I am grateful for this important and thought-provoking book.
Wendy Virgo, speaker and author

CATCHING CONTENTMENT

May you find treasure
in the depths of who
God is.

Blessings,

Liz Leo

CATCHING CONTENTMENT

HOW TO BE HOLY SATISFIED

LIZ CARTER

INTER-VARSITY PRESS
36 Causton Street, London SW1P 4ST, England
Email: ivp@ivpbooks.com
Website: www.ivpbooks.com

First published 2018

British Library Cataloguing-in-Publication Data
A catalogue record for this book is available from the British Library.

ISBN: 978–1–78359–740–6
eBook ISBN: 978–1–78359–741–3

Set in Dante 12/15 pt
Typeset in Great Britain by CRB Associates, Potterhanworth, Lincolnshire
Printed in Great Britain by Ashford Colour Press Ltd, Gosport, Hampshire

Inter-Varsity Press publishes Christian books that are true to the Bible and that communicate the gospel, develop discipleship and strengthen the church for its mission in the world.

IVP originated within the Inter-Varsity Fellowship, now the Universities and Colleges Christian Fellowship, a student movement connecting Christian Unions in universities and colleges throughout Great Britain, and a member movement of the International Fellowship of Evangelical Students. Website: www.uccf.org.uk. That historic association is maintained, and all senior IVP staff and committee members subscribe to the UCCF Basis of Faith.

For Tim
Thanks for cheering me on,
bringing me tea and being my home

And for T and N
Thanks for being you, and for letting me
tell annoying stories about when you were small

CONTENTS

ACKNOWLEDGMENTS

I thank my God every time I remember you.
In all my prayers for all of you, I always pray with joy
because of your partnership in the gospel from the first
day until now, being confident of this, that he who began
a good work in you will carry it on to completion
until the day of Christ Jesus.
Philippians 1:3–6

This book has been a long journey of incredible highs and quite a few aching lows. So many people have accompanied me on the journey in different ways.

First, I'd like to thank the team at New Wine. This book is your fault. You know who you are – thank you.

Thank you so much to the team at IVP for reading my long proposal and deciding to 'explore it further' with me. Those words will forever be etched on my heart! Thanks especially to my editor, Eleanor Trotter. Your gentle encouragement to murder darlings and clean up flabby bits has been both a learning curve and a blessing. Thanks for cheering me on and sending me turquoise stationery. Thanks also to Kath Stanton, my copy-editor, and the rest of the team for all your hard work.

To all my beta-readers, I'm so grateful for your words of encouragement and your prompts for improvement. Thank you to Dawn James, Brian Betts, Vicki Cottingham, Ali Grafham, Fiona Lloyd, Roy McCloughry, Zoe Heming and Janine Kennedy.

Thank you to Tanya Marlow and Catherine Campbell, and to Steve and Claire, for allowing me to use some of your stories. Your grace and courage have spoken to me more than I can say.

To my church family at All Saints, Wellington, what can I say? You've been Jesus to me so many times. You've visited me in hospital, prepared meals for me when I was sick (and much cake), made me a turquoise prayer shawl and sundry other knitted goods, and welcomed my family in. A special mention has to go to my lush Home Group (I wrote that in a Welsh accent, of course), the Revive Babes and Book Group Lovelies, the Faith Explored group and the mums' Bible study group. Thanks for being fabulous.

To all my dear friends from Priorslee and POD and G&T. You've been cheering me on for years, through some really difficult times. Thanks to the Mums' Lunchers – I know you don't believe all this stuff, but you support me and drink copious amounts of tea with me in all the cafés in Shropshire. You rock! Thanks also to my awesome Prayer Warriors – your support means everything.

Part of living with illness means there can often be a measure of loneliness, especially when housebound. For this, I am so grateful to my online friends and groups. Thank you to the MN Chatters/Pray-ers for keeping me going despite your bafflement at my worship preferences and love of GK. To all in Mrs and Mr V (you know who you are!). To Brussians, who get it and have warmed up my life, and Oct 03, who have been such a mainstay over the years. To all the talented authors in the Association of Christian Writers, who have been a huge encouragement.

So many of you have been a close personal support. I'd love to mention all my friends and family by name, but space prevents it. So write your name here >>   << and accept my warm thanks and love.

To Mum and Dad, Wallace and Mary Brown, who instilled a love of writing and editing in me when they wrote *Angels on the Walls* and used far too many exclamation marks. Thank you for your unconditional love and support over the years. You've always been my champions and my role models. Thanks also to my parents-in-law, Stephen and Gwyneth Carter. I feel so fortunate to have you as my PILs. To the rest of my wider family – I'm so blessed by you and love you all to bits.

To Tim, Tabitha and Nathaniel. You're my favourites. You bring out the best of me and challenge the worst. Thanks for enduring my writing gripes and reading my early drafts. Thanks for your red pen and for Saturday night silliness over *Britain's Got Talent* – even when Dad whizzes through the slushy bits. I love you all.

And finally, to Jesus. It's all for you. You're the one who held out contentment to me, and I will always be filled with bursting gratitude.

If you'd like to connect with me, please find me at my website: <www.greatadventure.carterclan.me.uk>
Facebook: <www.facebook.com/GreatAdventureLiz>
Twitter: @LizCarterWriter
Instagram: greatadventureliz

INTRODUCTION

*I have learned the secret of being content in any and
every situation, whether well fed or hungry,
whether living in plenty or in want.*
Philippians 4:12

Sam is breathless, giddy. Eyes fixed ahead on the red dot
speeding through the sky, growing and expanding as it hurls
itself through space. He stretches out his hands, arms flung
wide, face turned upwards, a picture of concentration.

Everything within him wants to catch the ball.

But his hands are in the wrong place. He's too far away. He
lurches over to the right, hands higher, zones in on the target,
every last ounce of energy concentrated on his goal.

The ball slams into his waiting hands. Bounces back out of
his grasp. He reels, pitches himself over, grasps the ball a split
second before it hits the ground, clasps his hands together
over it, holds it tightly to his belly.

Phew! He's done it. He's caught it.

He's caught it because he chased it. Because he reached
for it. Because he was focused and determined. Because he
wanted it so much.

This book is about catching something. Wanting it. Chasing
it. It's about embracing a treasure called contentment.

But may I begin by confessing something?

I don't always feel contented.

Sometimes I'm not sure what contentment even means. We're sold a version every day, everywhere we look, from adverts full of smiley folk around heaving tables enjoying life – and nice things – together, to people on our social media feeds living lives full of Insta-happiness, smiling perfect families framed in sepia supremacy.

When I'm faced with this version of contentment, I feel far from it.

You see, I am ill. Chronically ill. I have suffered from a rare lung disease all my life, with my lungs slowly deteriorating over the years. As well as general fatigue and breathlessness from day to day, I am afflicted with repeated chest infections, which can range from minor bronchial bugs to full-blown double pneumonia and pleurisy. Some sections of my lungs are collapsed, some enlarged and covered in scars. This leads to a life that can be narrow, existing within four walls for weeks at a time while my body struggles to cope with the strain. I also live with persistent pain, sometimes low-level, sometimes terrifying, agonizing misery. I sit and weep with it, not knowing what else to do.

So what does contentment mean for someone like me? It's a question I have asked myself many times.

And I'm wondering how contented you are feeling as you start this book. Are you at peace in your life? Or are you heavy with despair and brokenness? Perhaps you think that anyone who says that you could know any kind of contentment must be insensitive, because your life is in tatters and you think you'll never know peace again.

After all, contentment is for people who have everything they need. The TV says so.

It's not for people who have lost their dear husband or buried their child. It's for those who aren't fearful or tired or afraid. It's for those fortunate enough to be confident and productive and beautiful, for those who are not ill, not watching their life ebb away in waves of pain and exhaustion, wondering *why me?* Contentment is for people who have enough money, enough stuff, enough friends, enough acclaim. Peace comes to those who don't have fertility issues, who cuddle smiling newborns bundled in waffle blankets, those whose children live charmed lives.

But not to those whose child isn't neurotypical, whose child will never achieve the golden trophies of popularity and straight As, beauty and talent. It's not for people stumbling under a heavy blanket of blackness, depression weaving its tendrils around their deepest soul, or for those who live in loneliness so intense it clamps itself around them, squeezing in until there's nothing left.

So is contentment only for those who dance through life, unafflicted and unstricken, forever smiling for a world that loves them back?

That's something of how I used to see it.

I thought I was getting things wrong. Somewhere in the past I'd swallowed the line that Christians should be Shiny Happy People. Certain Christian books and articles had claimed that contentment was about happiness, and that being Christians should make us the happiest people on earth. But I didn't feel very shiny or very happy. I felt pain-filled and disappointed. I thought I was falling short of God's plan, that I should plaster a big smile on my face and demonstrate how happy Jesus was making me. When I failed to do this, I was failing God.

Because I found the idea of contentment difficult, I went on a journey of exploration. What does it really look like? I'd read the words of the apostle Paul in his letter to the Philippians, insisting he had discovered the secret to being content in every situation. Could that really be true? *Every* situation? I began to wonder if the contentment he was talking about looked completely different from contentment as I'd envisaged it.

The four Cs of contentment

This book is about transforming our understanding of the word 'contentment'.

On my quest to grasp what Paul was saying about finding contentment in Christ, I identified four areas shaping my thinking, drawing particularly from the book of Philippians, but also from other places in Scripture and from Christians' experiences down through the ages.

- Confident contentment: what does it mean to be confident in our faith, our identity, our hope and our future, and how does this help us take hold of peace in our lives right now?
- Courageous contentment: can we really experience the kind of contentment Paul is talking about, even in our most difficult times?
- Captivated contentment: does seeking God's face and God's glory help us to find serenity in our lives? What does it mean to be wholly satisfied in God?
- Contagious contentment: can an outward-looking attitude of heart create an intense sense of peace in us? Is it possible that in catching hold of contentment, we become catching *with* it?

Come and join me on this adventure.

This pursuit of something that God longs for all of us to find.

We will explore the deep contentment that can be found in Jesus, a different kind from the one we might normally think of. We can experience a holy satisfaction, which might not mean we will always *feel* wholly satisfied.

No, it doesn't necessarily look like that cat who got the cream. In fact, it may actually look like pain and suffering. Like living in a broken world.

Find moments of space as you read to reflect on what contentment means for you. I hope that something of what I share might resonate, and that you will catch hold of the kind of contentment that can only be found in knowing Christ. I pray that as you read, you will know God speaking to your heart, pouring love over you, whispering words of grace to your spirit and filling you with joy unspeakable.

I look into the mystery
Of this greatest of treasures;
I look with my doubt-filled heart,
My soul heavy with the weight of the world.
I search with eyes wide
And expectant soul,
Take a deep breath
And walk into the journey,
Place my shaky hand in yours,
Drag my tired feet forwards
Into the wild depths of you.

PART 1:
CONFIDENT CONTENTMENT

But blessed is the one who trusts in the Lord,
whose confidence is in him.
Jeremiah 17:7

Eat, drink and be merry, because this is all there is.
That's what they say.
No meaning.
No purpose.
Nothing.
So party while you can!
But then I bend under the weight
Of the mystery of me, unsolved,
Of the value of me, unmeasured.
Is God God? Is God good?
I reach for confidence through the leaden sky,
And see it hurled at me,
Peace beyond understanding
In doubt-tinged certainty.

1. CONFIDENT IN OUR FAITH

The light was too bright. It pounded at my pupils, sending my brain into a swirling fog. My limbs were stones, too heavy to move, and my breathing too short, too rapid, a band of iron clamped around my ribs. I couldn't speak.

'Hypoxemia. Sats in 70s. She needs oxygen.'

'IV morphine.'

'X-ray.'

The words spun through my head, making little inroad into my consciousness.

A sudden sense of falling away, flying out over the room, as the morphine snaked through my veins. A blessed relief.

'You have a pneumococcal infection in both lungs,' the consultant said to me later. I peered at him through heavy, aching eyelids. 'And you have a large build-up of fluid on both lungs too. Pleural effusions. We need to drain that off.'

Trying to breathe was like trying to drag heavy bricks upwards, and sharp knives stabbed my sides and my shoulders, cutting through me. My sats remained too low, even with oxygen. My husband sat with me, and we prayed.

'God, please take this pain away. Please. It hurts. It hurts too much.'

But the pain raged through me, battering every part.

God didn't take it away.

Over days and weeks I recovered to some extent, but the pain weighed heavily for a long time, and the memory of it rending my body in two haunted me. The long-term effects were even more of a problem. 'Your disease has spread,' my consultant told me after a CT scan. 'You have scarring across all your lobes. There's no point us doing that surgery now because it's too widespread.'

A faith besieged

I spoke with a friend online. I told her how, despite the pain, I had known God was close to me. But she couldn't see it. 'Why do you keep your faith when you experience something like that? Why are you so sure it's all true? God didn't step in and make you better, so why?'

The questions resonated, churning around in my mind and spirit. How could I be confident in a faith that didn't always seem reasonable and still allowed for suffering?

I was taken back to my time as an undergraduate, studying theology at a secular university. Friends on the course assured me that there was no way my faith would survive the four years of study. I'd finally recognize that everything I'd believed in was built on little but myth and superstition, and that I had been conditioned as a child to have an irrational faith in a non-existent being. I would be set free from the bonds of my religion. In addition to realizing how illogical faith was, I would wake up to the reality that God wasn't healing me, and so I shouldn't trust him at all, even if he did exist.

But a strange thing happened. I found that my faith in Jesus Christ as Saviour and Lord was strengthened and revitalized through study. Digging into the historical accuracy of the Scriptures, the writings of the early church, the theology of Paul and the reliability of the Gospels, I uncovered an intensity of truth which blew my mind. All along I was being bombarded by counter-arguments, mocked and belittled for being so deluded. Yet, by the power of the Holy Spirit in me, I discovered that my faith was built on even deeper foundations than I had imagined.

Alongside this, my disease was worsening. In my early twenties I was struggling to live a normal life because I was sick so often. Much of the teaching I was hearing at the time told me that I would be healed, that I just needed to exercise more faith.

More faith. But was it really that simple?

Doubt needs room to breathe

When healing didn't happen, confidence in my personal faith would slip and doubt creep in. Friends kept me supplied with good reasons to mistrust faith, but I felt that by letting doubt in, I was letting God down.

In his excellent book *Faith and Doubt* John Ortberg describes faith and doubt as two sides of a coin. 'There is a mystery to faith,' he writes, 'as there is to life, that I don't fully understand.'[1] Every soul, he believes, is perched on a fine line between faith and doubt. To doubt is human, and if we don't allow room for doubt, then we are in danger of being caught in a loop of unthinking faith. 'When people of faith are not willing to sit quietly sometimes and let doubt make its case, bad things happen.'[2]

If we don't listen to our doubts and address them, they will eat away at us, eroding any sense of certainty and setting us adrift once again. When my friend challenged my faith after my hospital stay, doubt rushed in. But I had a choice: I could brush it away and avoid thinking about it too much, or I could face it full on.

I thought about the questions my friend was asking me. Why did I keep faith when I was in such pain? When God didn't stop it? I wrote in my diary after I came home:

> I only remember calling out to God once, 'Why?' The answer was somehow in the silence and the struggle for every breath. In the recollection of Jesus' own agony. In the ministrations of the staff, in the love of my family and friends. No awesome glimpses of heaven or visions of angels. But a God who was next to me, in it with me, who knew.

I didn't experience miraculous healing, but the Holy Spirit of God brooded alongside me in my suffering, and I came out of that hospital even more confident in my faith than before, despite the racking pain which had almost consumed me and the utter weakness of my body. In my frailty I had nowhere else to go, and when I went to God, I found the everlasting arms spread far wider than even my acute distress.

Pondering the questions gave room for doubt to breathe, and in turn built faith in me. Greg Boyd suggests that we need to 'learn to live effectively in an ambiguous world where *why* questions can rarely if ever be adequately answered'.[3] In the hospital my *why* question was not answered, but my soul was gathered up in an ocean of love.

Rational, credible . . . and death-defeating

The Bible offers a rich resource for grounding our faith with reason. The further we explore, the bigger God becomes – and the more we see of his magnitude, creativity, love and power. If we use our God-given reason to delve deeply into why we believe, then we will find a firm rock to build our house on.

When besieged by doubt, I sometimes find it helpful to immerse myself in other Christians' thoughts, as well as soaking in God's Word. *But Is It Real?* by Amy Orr-Ewing, *The Reason for God* by Tim Keller and *Mere Christianity* by C. S. Lewis are great examples of faith-affirming books. The *Unbelievable?* podcasts on Premier Christian Radio – where Christians and atheists discuss their views – help establish faith in concrete facts and lived experience, essential when trying to build a robust faith in a world that rejects it.

When my confidence is lacking, I think carefully about why I believe what I believe. I delve into the comprehensive evidence for the life, death and resurrection of Jesus Christ, and I come away astounded every time by what I discover.

I explore the research on early life and the possibility of the existence of God, on the fine-tuning of constants in the universe, on the construction of DNA. I think about why we as humans have an inbuilt moral code that is unexplained by evolution alone: why do we believe there should be human rights? Why do we see each individual life as valuable?

I spend time reflecting on our human consciousness – where do our senses originate? Why do we think? How do we love? Are these simply chemical reactions formed through billions of years of evolution, or are they signs of God's image imprinted upon us – a people capable of loving relationship? What about creativity, art, music and beauty?

Although I'm not particularly scientifically minded, I'm repeatedly staggered by the way the cosmos works together, almost like it's woven together in a great plan . . .

The more I think on these things, the more confident I am that there is a loving and personal Creator of the universe, one who lovingly crafted humanity for relationship with God and one another, yet with the freedom to do as we choose. And the more I search, the more overwhelmed and amazed I am that the God who is the Creator of the universe loves us so much that he sent Jesus, his Son, to die for us, to defeat death and rise again in glory. Praise God!

Bedraggled, pathetic . . . and stubborn

Sometimes, though, reason isn't enough.

A solid foundation of knowledge about what we believe will help us when we are in situations where we need to live out our faith – or account for it. But confidence in our faith is more than a certainty about the theory of our faith. More even than an assurance that Jesus Christ lived, died and was resurrected on the third day. It's a confidence which starts at a soul-deep place – and a confidence which, in my experience, grows with pain, rather than fading as a result of it. Instead of being shrunken by difficulty, it thrives on the assurance that God is faithful and his promises are true. It might be bashed, but it grows anyway, like a plant battered by a catastrophic storm, bedraggled and pathetic-looking in the aftermath, but establishing even stronger roots as it flourishes with stubborn determination.

Jesus Christ is worthy of our confidence, and our experience of pain and brokenness in this life does not have to shatter that confidence. Sometimes it will get battered and bruised, but it does not need to be broken or destroyed.

Confidence is sitting in a prison cell

Paul wrote the New Testament book of Philippians from prison. This most likely took the form of a 'house arrest' in Rome – he was living in a house that he rented, and was granted a little freedom and allowed to speak about Jesus to the people who came to visit him. But he remained under armed guard at all times, unable to leave the house or speak publicly.

Paul was writing to encourage the church in Philippi, where the followers of Christ were being terrorized by persecution throughout the area. His letter addressed their agonizing experience of suffering – and even dying – for their faith. His joy in them was evident from the first verse, and he longed for them to know the confidence in their faith that he himself knew, while imprisoned, and yet so gloriously free.

Right at the start of this book, the letter in which Paul talks most about contentment, he links confidence in the Lord to struggle and suffering. His situation is stark, yet people have gained more confidence in their faith *because* of this:

> Now I want you to know, brothers and sisters, that what has happened to me has actually served to advance the gospel. As a result, it has become clear throughout the whole palace guard and to everyone else that I am in chains for Christ. And because of my chains, most of the brothers and sisters have become confident in the Lord and dare all the more to proclaim the gospel without fear.
> (Philippians 1:12–14)

Paul wrote several of his letters around this time, and many came to know Christ through him – including some of his guards. Those Christians around him became more confident in the gospel because they were witnesses of Paul's response to his desperate situation: they observed his joy and confidence in Christ, and they saw others being saved because of this. God worked through his painful situation to further the good news of salvation.

We too can be confident in our faith, even when we face adversity, even when we feel we are locked in a prison cell with no visible means of breaking free. Because God works in and through our circumstances. In and through the mess.

A God in the dust

In Hebrews confidence in God is also a key theme. In chapter 4 the author explores the idea of Jesus being our 'great high priest' – one who is able to sympathize with our weaknesses because he has lived among us. High priests were the gatekeepers to the Holy of Holies – only they could enter the most sacred place and represent others to God. Jesus came to shatter that barrier and bring God into the dust with us.

Jesus' representation of a God of compassion and love stood in stark contrast to cultural norms in Graeco-Roman society. The idea of a God who sympathized was indeed unique. Their 'gods' were set apart, dispassionate and full of wrath. Even the Hebrews themselves, while worshipping God as holy, righteous and merciful, would have struggled with the idea of an incarnate, immanent God. But this God blazed into humanity in outrageous passion, sharing their tears and calming their fears. More than that, this God suffered *with* them. The verb 'to sympathize' here is best expressed as 'to suffer along with'.

The writer is particularly concerned with the unique character of Jesus as he talks about him in such terms. When high priests were mentioned in Scripture before, they were not called great, or the Son of God. Jesus our High Priest is above the rest, glorious and powerful, and we can come before him with genuine certainty: 'Let us then approach God's throne of grace with confidence, so that we may receive mercy and find grace to help us in our time of need' (Hebrews 4:16).

Like Paul, the writer doesn't shrink away from the reality that we live with pain and brokenness, but instead gives us permission to run to the one who completely understands it, one tempted in every way that we have been, yet is without sin (verse 15). This is an exceptional and unprecedented aspect of our faith: God in flesh and blood; God incarnate. God in the dust with us, able to sympathize, suffering with us. And because of this, we can find grace when we need it. We find mercy when we mess up, confidence even in the shadows.

Confidence through the silence

God builds faith through Scripture, through reason, through encounter and through everyday experience. When I was suffering from that case of double pneumonia, I wasn't able to sit and read books about the origins of life. All I could do was take hold of what I had discovered in the past and apply it to what I knew about God, and trust that he was holding me tightly – even through the silence. The confidence I had built up in my faith became a reality in my darkest moments. There was nothing else but God, nothing else but divine depths to plunge into, to sink deeply, but never drown.

In my starkest pain I held on to confidence in the Lord, and discovered that confidence to be a bedrock to contentment.

Learning to live with doubt helped me to develop certainty, but it also took me back to a time when I doubted the deepest part of me, rather than my faith. A time when my identity was in ruins . . .

But that's another story.

Prayer

Father,
Please release in me a more profound confidence
in my faith.
Help me to grab hold of it in my most pain-loaded
seasons,
To discover you in those moments,
To know you, God, the Creator and the Sustainer,
To know with certainty that you, Jesus, God's Son,
came among us,
Died,
And rose again in glory.
Give me strength to seize hold of my faith with
confidence,
And catch contentment.
Amen.

Reflection

- Have you let doubt strip away your certainty?
- How much confidence do you have in God right now?
- Do you need to entertain the idea of *some* doubt in order to let it become part of your confidence? How will you do this? What do you need to do now, at the start of this journey, to move closer to contentment?
- Reflect for a while on Hebrews 4:16. What does approaching God's throne of grace with confidence mean to you, in your situation?

2. CONFIDENT IN OUR IDENTITY

As a teenager, I was bullied at school.

I had been a sickly child, pale and bespectacled, a vicar's daughter who actually believed all that gubbins. In my secondary school years the accusing words came thick and fast.

Ugly. Thick. Idiot. Will never amount to anything. No-one will ever want to date you. Four-eyes. Useless. Unpopular.

Being off school ill so frequently made it worse – I was pathetic as well as ugly. It wasn't only students; sometimes it was teachers too. I just wasn't trying hard enough, they said. My GCSE year was blighted by nasty cases of recurrent bronchitis, and I remember shuffling back into school after an entire half-term off sick to slow handclaps and a sarcastic 'Well done. Thank you so much for joining us' from my form tutor and suppressed sniggers from the other pupils.

The words and the looks slithered into my subconscious and began a script which was to become a heavy cloud for years to come, weaving increasing negativity around me as I would grow up and experience a world hostile to a physically weak person. I began to speak the script over myself until I couldn't see anything beyond it.

The words plunged me into negative cycles of behaviour. I was jealous of anybody and everybody, worried that no-one liked me, worried if a friend had another friend she might like more.

My identity disappeared into a narrow box, closing in on me, the script feeding itself repeatedly through my deliberate choice to remain hemmed in. By my mid teens I could only see the words.

Identity building – a flawed foundation

Despite having an incredibly loving and supportive family, I came to an almost subconscious understanding that I would need to earn people's – and God's – favour through what I *did* and not through who I was. Consequently, I became attached to the idea of a future career in teaching. I would be an encouragement to children who saw themselves as lesser: the bullied, the rejected: in short, the children like me. I wanted to give them value. Maybe I could redeem my own poor self-esteem through building up others?

So I trained as a primary school teacher, my four-year degree being somewhat blighted by repeated lung infections. I'd be fine, I told myself; I simply needed to get on with it. After a year out where I met Tim, my husband, I started work in a school in a very deprived area of Birmingham. There many of the children came from places so broken that I could only hope I might make some significant difference. I was delighted to see them enjoying learning and lighting up with the discovery that they had worth and value. I felt that I had realized my identity at long last: I was needed.

For five years I persisted in teaching until my lung disease degenerated to the point where teaching was no longer a viable option. Aged only twenty-eight, I faced a huge knock to my identity: if I wasn't a teacher any more, something I had attached myself to for so long, what was I? And who was I? This sense of purpose was ripped away, and I didn't understand. Surely this was what God had wanted me to do? I had been making a difference to these kids! Why didn't God just heal me so I could carry on?

At around that time I had my first baby and sank all my purpose into motherhood. But the old words still haunted me: I wasn't enough; I had to justify my existence at all times.

The God who doesn't say, 'What do you do?'

When my husband moved jobs to be the vicar of two churches, I found myself questioning my calling there too. In his previous post, a pioneer church plant, I had been leading alongside him and had felt very much 'called'. I had my place; I knew who I was supposed to be.

In the new role the pieces of my life were once more thrown up into the air, landing in unfamiliar places. I wondered who I was called to be, what I was called to do. And I also had to accept the stark reality that I was not actually able to 'do' a great deal, practically.

So what did that mean for my identity?

Again, I thought that a 'calling' would define me. Just like when I felt that teaching had defined me, and then being a mum. I was searching for something to make me worth it. The first question people asked on meeting me was often: 'So what do you do?' And sometimes, 'What will you do in the church?' It felt like my calling – or what I was 'supposed' to be doing – was the most important thing in the eyes of others. Wasn't that what mattered to God too?

Instead of looking at all the different ministries and frantically clutching at where I might 'fit', I would have been better advised to look at God. I had forgotten that it was only he who would give me worth.

A young man named St Francis of Assisi looked to God first, and his life made a massive impact on those around him, and has done on millions ever since. A rich lad given to wild living, he had a clear and powerful dream where he realized that he was doing life badly, and God was calling him back to his own country. This dream radically changed him. He found he was unable to enjoy his former partying lifestyle, so instead he started to pray. His sense of call was strong, but he didn't know what it was that God was calling him to do. The details took a long time to become clear, so he had to spend time in intercession, looking to God. One day he found himself engulfed in God's presence. His biographer, Thomas of Celano, writes, 'Then it was that divine grace came upon him . . . Suddenly, he was inundated with such a torrent of love, submerged in such sweetness, that he stood there motionless, neither seeing nor hearing anything.'[1]

After meeting with God in this immersive way, he discovered that nothing else would satisfy him. A sense of contentment was heavy on him *before* he knew what God was calling him to do. It didn't matter if he had a specific calling or not, and it didn't matter what that calling was. What mattered was his attitude to God and his commitment to seeking God's will.

Filled with uncertainty about my future, it wasn't helpful to spend time immersing myself in that uncertainty. Instead of waiting for a calling to define me, I should have spent more time in God's presence, as Francis did.

But that doesn't mean me, surely?

'God loves you. Delights in you. Thinks you're brilliant,' said the speaker at an event I attended as a teenager. I shook my head. *No. Not me.* Somehow these words wouldn't override the older script which had me in its vice grip, to mix my metaphors. They must mean everyone else. God doesn't see me like that, because, frankly, I'm not worth seeing like that.

The trouble was that living under this cloud of false belief about my identity meant that I couldn't take hold of contentment, because I wasn't confident at all in who I was in Christ. Yes, I carried a kind of certainty about who I was, but that certainty was in my failings, my weakness, my uselessness as a person. My true identity was robbed from me by others' words and by my own decision to live under the influence of those words. Instead of reaching out to catch contentment, I grasped these negative words tightly to my chest until they became a part of me.

What I didn't do was listen to the words God spoke about me through the Bible. Words about value and freedom, love and worth.

No such word as worthless

Recently I was sick in hospital and on my ward was a woman called Rose[2] who lives with dementia, unable to speak. She lay in the corner, her hands fumbling with a red rubber ball. As a nurse went over to replace her oxygen mask, Rose threw the ball straight at her. She was shocked, then laughed and threw it back. 'Fabulous aim, Rose! Did you play cricket in your younger days?'

Rose threw the ball back, and a game began. Gradually, a few other nurses and health care assistants gathered around the bed and joined in. 'She's smiling, look,' one of them enthused, leaning in to stroke Rose's arm.

They began to speak to her, words of love and compassion, telling her how lovely she was, how much fun she was. I could see her shoulders shaking with laughter as they continued the ball game, her sallow face now lit up.

They took ten minutes in the middle of a busy day to say, 'Yes. You are valuable. You have worth. You are not a burden.'

The nurses were accentuating Rose's dignity by delighting in who she was and enjoying her playfulness, not simply treating her as a passive recipient of pity or compassion. They reminded me of how God imbues each one of us with infinite value, and takes pleasure in who we are, rather than in what we are able – or not able – to do. We are not worthless to God – no way.

A while ago a friend lost his job and was unable to find another one. 'I feel like I've lost myself,' he said. 'Like I'm an empty shell. Everything I am was bound up in that job . . . I just feel lost. Worthless.' In such a dark place it is difficult to embrace the truth of words from Scripture. But it's also in that dark place where, if we allow it, those words of infinite power rush in and pound away at the walls we have built around ourselves. Words which express God's wild love for us, his delight in us, his creativity reflected in us, and our glorious identity as valued children of the King.

But so many of us, like my friend above, live in the brokenness of shattered identity, and we cannot reach for contentment because we have no confidence in who we are.

Identity building – the Paul foundation

Do you hold on to a negative belief about yourself and find it difficult to read words in the Bible affirming who you are?

Perhaps a loving friend reminds you of Ephesians 2:10, and the words 'You are God's handiwork' impress themselves on your mind. But they fail to sink into your heart, because what you see in the mirror cannot possibly be God's handiwork. You nod and smile, but inside you are like ice, because it cannot mean you, surely.

Exploring the context of passages like this one can help the words permeate our souls. Paul included the words that we find in Ephesians 2:10 as part of a longer section addressed to the new believers in Ephesus about God's saving grace. In the previous verses, he reminded us, as followers of Christ, that we are saved not through our own actions or by how good we are, but by the riches of God's grace which have been expressed through the sacrificial kindness of Jesus on the cross. Because of this, we have no excuse to boast in ourselves – or, in fact, to do ourselves down. God has accomplished this incredible saving work in us because of his great love for us. This is the grounding of our identity: not what we do, but what God does in us, and God's creativity reflected in us.

The Greek word for 'handiwork' or 'workmanship' here translates as something like 'poem' or 'work of art' – God's grace has transformed us and led us into all we were created to be, which is something beautiful. We are 'created in Christ Jesus to do good works, which God prepared in advance for us to do'. We are fulfilled in the riches of God's grace – what better identity could there ever be?

God's delight in us is grounded in his saving love for us, a love that overcomes all our wrongs and forgives us with fervent grace. Our identity in God is firm and true: God is for us, and delights in the restoration of our relationship.

So yes – this *does* mean you. You are God's handiwork, loved and restored, and not by your own efforts, but simply by God's all-consuming, passionate love for you.

Yet it is difficult to search for who we are in Christ in a society so totally obsessed with 'finding ourselves'. We have built a tendency to navel-gaze – we look inwards rather than outwards, downwards rather than upwards. We think that we can solve all our problems by looking inside ourselves. And then we fail, and our identity takes another hit.

The apostle Paul gave us a new understanding of identity. Instead of looking inwards, we should take on a radically different mindset: 'I have been crucified with Christ and I no longer live, but Christ lives in me. The life I now live in the body, I live by faith in the Son of God, who loved me and gave himself for me' (Galatians 2:20).

Let's unpack this a little. In Paul's letter to the Christians in Galatia, he was most concerned with a group of people who were trying to persuade everyone else that they should be bound by the Jewish ceremonial laws – the very opposite of the message of freedom in Christ that Paul had been communicating. He was assuring the Galatians that they were justified through faith and not through the law. In the previous verse Paul said that he had died to the law – that the law had lost all power over him, because he was now in Christ. When he talked about being crucified with Christ, he obviously wasn't saying that he'd physically died with Christ on the cross, but that he had put to death all those things which had had power over him – over his old self. All his selfishness, greed, ambition and longing after power were nailed to the cross, and so lost their power over his mind, body and spirit, because of Christ's great triumph on that cross. Paul was saying that he couldn't do this on his own: he couldn't conquer his own sinful nature, but he needed to surrender these things to Jesus.

Paul's new take on identity is that when we surrender everything we have to Christ – to the extent of nailing to the cross all those things which would separate us from him – our core identity comes into its fullest expression. In looking upwards, we run headlong into who we were created to be.

He explains this further in what follows: 'I no longer live, but Christ lives in me.' For Paul, our worth comes in setting aside the 'I', doing away with our old selves who were so very insistent on being so very important. When we put ourselves aside and allow Christ into our daily lives, in all the niggly aspects, all the irritations, the exhaustion, the bickering and the disappointments, we will find ourselves more fulfilled as humans than we ever could do by relying on something or someone else for our sense of self-worth.

We don't need to find ourselves, because you know what? We are already found. Gloriously found and loved and cherished. What more worth do we need? The truth of who we are in Christ can speak even to a young bullied sick girl who thought she was useless.

Embrace your identity in Christ

In embracing confidence about who we are in Christ, we can seize hold of a depth of contentment we will never find if we believe the destructive words that others – and Satan, the enemy – speak over us. For many of us, this may be a long and painful process of active refusal to descend into our old scripts and a determination to live in the truth of what God says, and for some of us there will be a holy moment where we are bathed in the knowledge of how God sees us.

That young bullied sick girl lived too long with a sense of failure and uselessness. It was only later on that she would discover who she really was.

Ironically, we embrace our identity in Christ when we become no longer 'I'. We become more fully the person God dreamed up when we were made, and in so doing we catch hold of confident contentment.

But is that enough? We might be confident in our identity right now as loved children of the King, but how do we hold on to the hope that Christ has given us?

Prayer

Father,
Release me into my identity in you.
May I know my worth in you,
Not in how productive or attractive
Or talented or useful I am.
Make me aware of any negative script
I am stumbling under the weight of,
And tune my inner words
To the truth you speak over me.
Help me to be confident in who I am
As your child,
Whatever situation I face.
To be confident that you have called me out
    of darkness
Into your marvellous light.
May I catch hold of a new sense of contentment
Within my glorious identity as an heir of your
    kingdom.
Amen.

Reflection

- Where is your identity – have you built it the flawed way or the Paul way?
- What does your internal script sound like?

- You may find it helpful to write down some of the words you hear, then screw up the paper and throw it away, and write down God's truth instead. You might also reflect on this list of 'truth statements' produced by the Freedom in Christ Discipleship Course, which takes the old negative words and replaces them with God's Word: <https://ficm.org/wp-content/uploads/2013/04/Truth-About-Me.pdf>.
- Have you been so busy trying to find yourself that you've lost the truth of who you really are: an outrageously loved child of God? How will you take time to absorb yourself in that truth?
- Reflect for a time on Ephesians 2:4–10. Let these words saturate your soul and replace any negative words you have been holding close. You may have to take some time to think and pray over this if you have lived for a long while with a scarred identity. Be kind to yourself, and remember that you are God's work of art, and God longs to lead you into his amazing freedom.

3. CONFIDENT IN OUR HOPE

The first thing I noticed about my new friend Steve[1] was that his face shone with God's presence.

Only after that did I notice the signs of Parkinson's disease.

When we were introduced, Steve said to me, 'I just love Jesus.' He held a Bible close to his heart, and later told me he took a version of it everywhere: 'Once upon a time I saw the Bible as a book, then later as a manual for life, then later still as real life itself, and now as a beating heart, fusion with the very presence of God.'

Steve grew up in church, his father a well-known preacher in evangelical circles. His dad was incredibly busy with church and with other people. Steve lost himself in the busyness of church as well, rushing from one thing to another, from kids' work to leading groups, preaching to worship, leadership to stacking chairs. He was living a sincere Christian life, on the outside strong and secure in his faith. But deep down, he tells me, he carried a raw pain, a sense that something wasn't right. Somewhere along the way he had lost confidence in his faith and his identity, and in his hope in God. Part of it was the difficulties he had with his father, the successful pastor who Steve felt had more time for others than for him. Steve was living in the wounded hope that being seen as spiritually involved in church would gain his father's approval.

Shaky foundations and a shocking diagnosis

His pain came to a head and he left the church. From the outside looking in, he found himself asking two questions.

First, was the God of the universe really there, and, by his Holy Spirit, inside him? If so, he needed to make significant changes. He couldn't look at himself at that moment and say that he was living a Jesus-centred life. In fact, he struggled to find any significant differences in the way he was living his life from the behaviour of people without faith. He was worried, anxious, discontented. What he was living, he tells me, was a compromised lifestyle. In the times when he really needed God, he reached out, and God in grace blessed him. But everything remained on Steve's terms: 'I viewed myself as alive in Christ, but underneath there was a deeper problem. No firm foundations, no conviction of the truth.'

The second question he asked himself was about the Bible: were there really overarching, eternal truths running through it? And, if so, why did his life not seem to match up to it? People reminded him of Bible verses and words that they felt God might be speaking into his life, which he read but then placed aside. He didn't understand where God was in all his pain.

At the same time as Steve was wrestling with all this, he was given a diagnosis of Parkinson's disease, an illness affecting nerve cells in the brain, causing symptoms of tremors and muscle weakness. There is no cure. 'I sat in the car and cried with Claire,'[2] he says. 'I remember telling her that I had to make the most of my life, that God had plans for good, but feeling so scared.'

What spoke most clearly to Steve in this time of uncertainty was the reaction of his wife. Claire, struggling herself with Steve's lack of confidence in God and the new diagnosis, listened, respected and honoured him in his darkness. Her witness – her quietness of spirit – was what opened up his heart.

Confident through damage and ravage

Over the following months and years, Steve experienced a complete transformation in his relationship with God. In his newly diagnosed disease, he did not succumb to discontentment, but instead chose to exercise confidence in God. He was awakened by hope. Eventually, he returned to church, and he 'lived a hugely different life . . . But it's brilliant.'

He came to be certain that Christ was in him and for him, and that because of that he was whole, despite the degeneration caused by his disease and the weakness of his body. He described how God ministered to him in a difficult time: 'I experienced what I can only describe as "shalom". Utter peace. No good thing withheld. It was truly amazing.'

While the disease ravaged his body, he chose not to define himself by the disability, but instead by the freedom and healing he found in Jesus. Steve was not physically healed, despite much prayer, but found something at an even more profound level, something of God's grace extended in his raw brokenness, which released a kind of contentment. Instead of being caged in bitterness, he was confident in the love of God. Claire says, 'When everything is stripped away, that's when you see what's really important. That's when you see God.'

'I do sometimes ask God why I haven't been healed,' Steve shares. 'But I've come to understand that I've been wonderfully healed in my spirit, my emotions, and actually in my relationship with my father as well. I know that I don't have to wait for the time when I might be physically healed, because I know the presence and power of God so much. I'm confident that I'm loved.'

Steve describes contentment as 'total intimacy and relationship with God. There's nothing else. You know you're very precious, but you're not *it*. He's it. He's in you. He's united with you. It feels like you're floating on this huge ocean of God's utter peace.'

When asked about the anxiety he used to experience, he tells me that he sometimes feels it still. Living a life confident in God doesn't mean a life that's always free from worry. But when he starts to struggle, he makes an active decision to obey God's Word, and instead of bowing under worry, brings it before God's throne in prayer, with thanksgiving. 'Living in each moment is a choice to be in God's presence.'

Steve and Claire have become confident in their hope despite what they are living through, and because of this they know a fullness of life beyond imagining. Their unshaking assurance challenges me, because it's sometimes all too easy to sound like you are confident in God, when underneath you are rocked with uncertainty. This couple's confident contentment is deeply authentic, and yet born of pain.

'Prosperity' as a fridge magnet

I was once challenged about my own depth of confidence in hope when a woman made a beeline for me at the end of a meeting. I'd seen her looking at me during the worship session, and noticed how she was frowning, as if puzzled, when I failed to stand and sing. 'God has given me a word for you,' she said, and I smiled at her. It takes courage to speak of God's Word to people. 'He has given me a verse from Jeremiah,' she continued. I immediately knew what it would be. I smiled again, and tried not to grit my teeth too hard. 'God said that he has plans to prosper you. Not to harm you. To give you hope and a future. You don't need to worry, because he is going to prosper you! You can step into your inheritance of hope!'

I smiled and thanked her, with all genuineness, but inside I stored this up with all the other times I had been given the same verse with the same promises. Now, I love the Word of God and love that God has spoken through verses of Scripture again and again, to countless millions throughout history, and continues to do so today. God speaks to me through Bible passages in stimulating and fresh ways all the time. But I wonder if we sometimes take God's Word too lightly, or too much at face value? If we spend time meditating on it, giving it the depth of consideration it is due, it can be a significant step to contentment when times are tough, because this kind of faithful reading increases our confidence.

I love the verse from Jeremiah which I referred to above: ' "For I know the plans I have for you," declares the LORD, "plans to prosper you and not to harm you, plans to give you hope and a future"' (Jeremiah 29:11). Alluring, hope-drenched words. But are they sometimes used too casually, almost as a sticking plaster when we find ourselves in difficulty? *I'm struggling, but it's OK, because God has plans to prosper me.*

With this verse, as with any other, it is vital to look at the context. When these words are used as an 'everything's going to be fine' bookmark or fridge magnet, we should remember that they were written to the exiles imprisoned in Babylon, prophesying of a time in the future when God would gather them and bring them home to Jerusalem – seventy years from then. And even then, things wouldn't suddenly become perfect – they would return to a city devastated, a rebuilding project that would take many, many years and would be a harrowing, uncomfortable period for them. So what did God mean by telling the exiles of plans to prosper them and not to harm them, to give them hope and a future?

Hang on in there – that rebuilding plan is in action

God did indeed have plans for their good.

Jeremiah was breathing hope to people in a most desperate position, people far from home and persecuted for their beliefs, people who knew they would never again see their homeland. But instead of promising them that God would get them out of it, Jeremiah turned the thinking of this world on its head by counselling the exiles to accept their lives under Babylonian rule, and to submit to the authorities there – even to pray for the prosperity of their neighbours. To settle where they were, but all the time to keep hold of their certainty that God had their future as a nation at heart. Jeremiah didn't give them false hope by promising that this future would be theirs for the taking right now in their lives; instead he advised them to comply with, and participate in, this situation. He wasn't always much loved among his contemporaries for this kind of advice, but his words touched the lives of those who decided to live in ambiguity, balancing their calling to put down roots and thrive where they were with that future of restoration they were promised. Jeremiah was, in essence, giving the same advice as Paul: be assured of God's glorious hope for the future, and flourish in that hope where you are now – even if that looks like a prison cell.

Jeremiah was teaching the Israelites about confident contentment.

The words of verse 11 would have carried the exiles through some of the hardest times, always holding on to the knowledge that God would deliver their nation, that there was hope and a future for their descendants. And this came to pass in the most remarkable of ways, with Nehemiah and Ezra beginning work on the rebuilding project in around 448 BC. Many passages from the Old Testament express the exultation of this time, with Jerusalem bursting into joyous life as the ancient ruins were rebuilt. The sense of hope pervades these verses – God's plan being fulfilled.

It is possible that we have made verses like Jeremiah 29:11 a kind of talisman. And then it is no wonder that we struggle when it does not seem to be fulfilled in our life, when there is little evidence of us prospering, of us not being harmed. Many of the exiles *were* harmed, but held these words dear as a promise for their nation's future. I wonder if people who quote this verse to those going through dark times, without careful thought and prayer, are sometimes a bit like Job's comforters: well intentioned, but possibly damagingly wrong? God was extending hope to those in a horrendous situation, but not making a promise that life would suddenly become free of difficulty. We find a much more profound way of holding these words close to our hearts if we understand that the reality is we are broken, and may not be fully 'fixed' in our lifetimes, but that nevertheless God's plans are always for good for us.

'You don't need to worry, because he is going to prosper you. You can step into your inheritance of hope!' the woman said to me, in a generosity of spirit that I could only be blessed by. And, actually, her words were true. God will prosper me and does give me an inheritance of hope. In recognizing that this does not always mean that I will see great changes in my circumstances today or tomorrow, but that it does always mean I can trust in God's ultimate plan, I come to a confident place in the middle of my pain, a place where I smile back at the woman and say in all truth, *Yes, God does. Yes, I believe it.*

All of us are looking for something to hope for, and hope sparks us into life. But the most beautiful of all hopes is to be found in the hope of glory – the hope of all being made right at last. It's to that hope we will turn next.

Prayer

Father God,
When I wonder what your plan is,
Why I am left desolate,
Remind me of the hope that sparks life,
Streaming through the darkness,
Drawing me to glorious light.
Thank you that you have given me a hope
   and a future,
That you are with me in my present.
Help me to find confidence in you where I am,
Flourish in your present hope,
And catch contentment.
Amen.

Reflection

- How does the example of Steve and Claire speak to you?
- How could you move closer to accepting God's ultimate mandate for your good, not for harm, even when all the evidence leads you to question this?

- Reflect for a while on Jeremiah 29:1–14. Ask God to speak to you as much through the preceding verses as well as verse 11. What do you think God is saying to you about hope?

4. CONFIDENT IN OUR FUTURE

I asked my consultant what my future might look like.

'It's hard to say, really,' she said, putting her pen down and meeting my eyes. 'Many people with your condition live a long life, but some are reliant on oxygen later on. And some end up on the transplant list.'

I swallowed. 'Might that be me?'

'Your disease is moderately severe – your lungs have degenerated a great deal over the years. Continuing at this rate, I'd say it's a possibility. But not for many years, so try not to worry.'

I try not to worry, but it is so difficult when infection strikes yet again, another hit on the lungs, another scar to add to the rest. The pain grows worse as I grow older, and the future looks bleak. Sometimes I think too much, letting the possibilities play out through my anxious mind. I think about the narrow confines already placed around my life, and wonder what it will be like when these margins are tightened more and more. Will I lose all my mobility? Will I ever leave my house? Be able to talk with friends? Even now, when I am sick, talking is hard. Inside me there is a river of yearning, a desperation to be heard, an ocean of meaningful words. But they stay there, battened down and imprisoned by my body. 'I'm a bit better,' I mutter out loud, and that's not even true.

So what do I have to look forward to, in the years to come? Do I even have years to come?

Curse the dying light

In the UK we are quiet around death. Funerals are sombre affairs; we dress in black and go as low-key as we can. It has become our way of coping with mourning. In some non-Western cultures a funeral may be more vibrant, more of a celebration of the loved one's life. Some say that this is a healthier approach, that we do not talk enough about death, that we suppress it because we are afraid of it.

We fear death more nowadays for a number of reasons. Historically, life was cheaper, in the sense that earlier death was more common. Most families lost at least one child; people didn't live as long; common ailments were often terminal. This didn't make death any less tragic, but it made it more normalized, and so people didn't minimize the effects. They viewed grieving as a necessary and routine part of life.

Now we are in the fortunate position of living in a society where medicine has taken great leaps forward, where common childhood illnesses have been all but stamped out, where people live healthier lives for longer. Death, therefore, has become more of a mystery to us, more of a horror. We see death as repugnant, offensive and oppressive, an unnatural and hideous thing. We hide it away and pretend it's not really there.

But we fear death also because we place a high value on people, and we place a high value on people because we are made in God's image. In every culture and every society and every faith system this image is reflected when we rage against death, because we know that every person possesses a value beyond words. And we rage all the more when we love a person dearly, because we were created for love, and love is the most profound reflection of God's image.

Many people have rejected the concept of an eternal life, and without that hope to cling to, they may fear death even more. There is nothing beyond, it is said, so we must hold on to what we have now, and when that slips away, there is nothing.

Dreaming of a Something

When I am racked with pain, I sometimes dream. I dream of eternity, of the hope of being all we should be, and the world being restored, with no more pain, no more sorrow, no more suffering. I dream about what it might feel like to live in a body which does all it should, a body without pain and fatigue, a body infused with strength and powered by living with the Creator of all things for all time. I get excited when I imagine not only my own freedom, but liberation for the world, our suffering, oppressed, groaning earth. No more cancer. No more motor neurone disease. No more dementia. No more depression. No more tears.

No more death.

Because there is indeed a something. In the gospel narrative our lives do not end in a meaningless nothing. Instead, we are assured of a certain future – God created us with life in mind, and offers us that life if we accept it. Perhaps one of the reasons why we are so repulsed by death is that God created us for life and therefore imbues us with hope for life and disgust for death. But hope for eternity doesn't mean that we have no need of mourning those we love who die. Jesus mourned. One of the most poignant and powerful verses in the Bible sums up Jesus' grief when his dear friend Lazarus died: 'Jesus wept' (John 11:35). We still rage against death for our dear ones, for God placed love deep in our souls, but we have something more to hold to. We know that there will be more – gloriously, beautifully, unimaginably more.

But what of now? What of our future, when this life is harrowing, even excruciating – and how does being confident of our ultimate future help?

Hope and Wii games

My children have always needed a lot of convincing that their rooms should be tidy. When they were small, the results of my instruction to tidy up would vary dramatically – depending on what they would get out of it. One day I would tell my son to tidy his room and say nothing more, and he might kick a few pieces of Lego under his bed and stuff some clothes into his wardrobe but leave his bed unmade and random bits of paper all over the floor. The next day I would tell him to tidy his room – 'And after that, we can play on the Wii together!' He'd bolt up the stairs like a rocket, hurling the Lego into its box, the clothes in the (almost) correct drawers, the paper in the bin, the bed (kind of) made.

A hope I had given him for his 'future' made a difference to his behaviour in the present. He held on to a promise of something good, and so went through the motions of something he found hard, with a smile on his face.

Author and pastor Tim Keller writes about the African-American 'spirituals' many people in slavery used to sing, songs which cry out Christian belief in a day of judgment, when everything will be made right. These songs have sometimes been criticized as being too other-worldly; they didn't help slaves develop any kind of self-sufficiency. Keller goes on to say,

> Imagine how ludicrous it would have been to sit down with a group of early nineteenth-century slaves and say, 'There will never be a judgment day in which wrongdoing will be put right . . . when you die, you simply cease to exist. Our only hope for a better world lies in improved social policy. Now, with these things in mind, go out there, keep your head high, and live a life of courage and love. Don't give in to despair.'[1]

The hope of these people in slavery – for a future of justice as well as one with no more pain and suffering – was, in fact, the reason for their decision not to give in to despair. Their plaintive songs became a rallying call and reminder for one another of a confident hope which underpinned their very survival in such hideous, inhumane circumstances. We all carry that desperation for justice to be done, that hope for everything finally to be put right. Their hope of being called home carried them through the unspeakable terror of their lives. This hope has carried millions and millions of others through the ages, and continues to do so today.

Hope in God's plans for our future – and for justice and mercy to prevail – deepens our contentment, should we actively choose to spread out our hands and catch it, and then live every day as if we believe it from our hearts.

Strangers in a strange land

The reality is that we are strangers in an alien land, and we are looking for home.

In Philippians chapter 3 Paul writes that our citizenship is in heaven. Now, the people of Philippi saw their Roman citizenship as vital, and held it close as part of their identity, so Paul using this heavily loaded word 'citizenship' about heaven may well have come as a shock to the Christians. But Paul doesn't mean that we should be so focused on heaven that we take our minds off earth. Tom Wright reminds us that the idea of 'citizenship in heaven' doesn't mean that we should forget about everything else, but rather that we should be thinking more in terms of 'colonies of heaven';[2] in other words, our purpose is to bring the kingdom to where we are now, just as the Romans were establishing Roman rule in Philippi.

Interestingly, Paul's letter to the Philippians is full of advice to rejoice in the Lord, something that is intertwined with the reality of suffering and death. Paul is aware that many of these fledgling believers will face persecution, and so gives them the gift of the words that they need, words that meet their pain face on and yet bring a sense of longing for what will eventually be. Paul knows that waiting for the kingdom to come – waiting with longing and yearning for heaven – can indeed bring contentment. But more than that, he advocates living the life of the future kingdom now: living for Christ alone, our minds and hearts set on Christ alone.

The valley of tears

Waiting and hoping for eternity with God is not like some intense teenage crush that brings nothing but heartbreak and emptiness.

It's not an unrequited longing, but instead an assurance of God's unmitigated and passionate return of love to us. In Psalm 84 the writer – someone obviously familiar with the temple – paints a poignant picture of longing for home, and of that longing being a sustaining place in difficulty. He recognizes God's dwelling place as where his heart is most at ease. 'My soul yearns, even faints, for the courts of the LORD,' he says, crying out his desperation to be in this place (verse 2). In verses 5–7 he describes a journey of pain, a passing through the 'Valley of Baka' (or valley of tears), which will be made 'a place of springs' and where the pilgrim will 'go from strength to strength'. For this psalmist, our life on earth is this valley, and we can be sustained through worship and spending time in the presence of God while living here.

The writer brings us back to his heartfelt cry with an alluring line of poetry expressing his longing to be with God: 'Better is one day in your courts than a thousand elsewhere' (verse 10). This line catches at my spirit, a plaintive sigh of longing to be in God's presence, which is better than anywhere else. The writer is probably banished to the wilderness, forlorn in his desire to be in the place he knows is his soul-home, yet somehow filled with peace *because* of that desire. The poem ends with an affirmation that those who trust in God are blessed – the psalmist knows that in the longing for his future home there can be a contentment in the here and now, because the longing is not in vain.

The acute homesickness of confident waiting

But how can this be? Surely longing for something means we are not yet satisfied – if we are waiting for something, we do not yet possess it. And waiting for death is hardly a recipe for happiness!

But longing for heaven isn't about waiting for death or even beckoning death. It's about homesickness. There is a deep ache in our soul which points to our real home. In Philippians chapter 1, Paul shares his struggle between longing to go to be with Christ and staying to encourage the believers. He writes that 'to live is Christ and to die is gain', and his desire is 'to be with Christ, which is better by far' (Philippians 1:21, 23). He is torn between the two, but knows that God is calling him to stay and to witness to the glorious gospel which has been revealed to him.

One of the most vital points Paul is making is that both living and dying are all about Christ. Living in the now, with all its difficulties and its joys, is all for Christ, and dying is even better, because Paul will at last be with Christ. His longing for this fuller knowledge of Christ helps him to focus on living as an apostle of Christ in the here and now. He is completely confident in the wonder of eternity with Christ, but also knows how to burrow deep into that hope – that ache for home – and so live in contentment in his painful present.

I wonder if you feel hopeful about eternity. Heaven is something that has been so twisted in art, literature and films, full of grumpy pious people and angels with harps, that we can easily carry around a skewed picture of what it means to spend eternity with Christ. There are so many questions about what 'heaven' will be – will our loved ones be there? What will we do? It is too mind-blowing even to try to imagine what eternity will look like. The Bible isn't clear on this, but we catch enthralling glimpses through some of the words of prophecy: thousands upon thousands of angels gathering around the throne, every creature in heaven and on earth bowing in reverence (Revelation 5). But the greatest thing – and the thing which Paul is so excited by and so centred on – is that we will be with Christ. Fully whole at last, surrounded by enchanting, astounding glory. Better by far!

It's important to remind ourselves that God is so much bigger than we can ever imagine. God is outside space and time. He created space and time. Eternity won't be anything we can conjure up in our human imaginations. It will be far better, far bigger, far wilder, far more beautiful. It will be beyond our wildest dreams. C. S. Lewis shared a poignant picture of eternity in *The Last Battle*, as the children came to the realization that they had died in their 'real' life, and were on the very verge of the discovery of Aslan's country:

> The term is over: the holidays have begun. The dream is ended: this is the morning . . . But for them it was only the beginning of the real story. All their life in this world and all their adventures in Narnia had only been the cover and the title page: now at last they were beginning Chapter One of the Great Story which no one on earth has read: which goes on for ever: in which every chapter is better than the one before.[3]

Aslan explains that all that had gone before – Narnia, and the children's home back in England – were all shadowlands, only weak copies of the reality, like an imprint of the better things to come. Aslan's country, where they have finally arrived, is the apex, the real deal, the place where the characters become completely liberated, where everything is as it should be.

We don't yet know what eternity will look like, but we sometimes catch enticing glimpses: a moment of beauty, listening to an awe-inspiring piece of music, standing on a mountaintop, or when staggered by the love we feel for another person. We might catch a shadow of the reality when we experience God's gift of peace, when we turn from our failings and follow Christ. We don't know what eternity will be like, but we do know that our God is a God of transformation, and promises to renew the heavens and the earth, to bring just rule to our world and to wipe away all evil. Paul didn't know what eternity would look like, but he knew that it would be with Christ, and that was all he desired and all he needed to know.

Christ was always enough.

We don't know what we will look like in eternity, but we can dream of freedom and justice, and shape those dreams into our prayerful, dynamic existence now. And Christ will always be enough for us – overwhelmingly, immensely enough.

When I think about the possibility of a lung transplant or an even more caged life, I can choose to slip into the despair of my lived reality, or instead enter into the hope of God's promises, promises which have never let me go. I ache for home, like the psalmist, and long for eternity with Christ, like Paul, and choose to let this ache, this homesickness, become joy within me. One of my favourite hymns is Charles Wesley's 'And Can It Be?', and I think one of the reasons why it resonates with me is because of the declaration in the final verse. 'No condemnation now I dread,' it proclaims, reminding me of the price Jesus has paid for me:

> Jesus, and all in Him, is mine!
> Alive in Him, my living Head,
> and clothed in righteousness divine.

What an incredible story. But it's the last line I love most, because it sums up this hope we hold, a hope which carries us through our valleys and over our mountaintops:

> Bold I approach the eternal throne,
> and claim the crown through Christ my own.

We stride into our future with great confidence, knowing that heaven is cheering us on by name, and more than that, knowing that we will at last see Jesus face to face. We can be confident in our future, a future that looks like the greatest adventure we could possibly imagine, both here on earth and into eternity.

But here on earth we know that the great adventure can be a long slog, and catching contentment in the day to day can be an elusive quest. So how does it work in action – in real life? How do we find courage for the journey?

Prayer

Dear Jesus,
Help me to be sure and certain
Of my future hope in you.
To know that to live is you, and to die is gain.
Assure me that eternity with you will be more
    incredible,
More astounding,
More beautiful than I can ever imagine.
May I ache for your courts,
Long for the story which will go on for ever,
And be assured of my room in your house,
A place prepared for me,
As your precious child,
Redeemed and loved.
Amen.

Reflection

- What are your thoughts and dreams about your future?
- Do you have confidence in spending eternity with Christ? What do you think that might look like?

- Reflect on Psalm 84. Think about the stark longing the writer shares, a longing which, while bringing an acute ache to his soul, also draws him into peace with God. How does this psalm speak to you?

PART 2:
COURAGEOUS CONTENTMENT

We are hard pressed on every side, but not crushed;
perplexed, but not in despair; persecuted, but not abandoned;
struck down, but not destroyed.
2 Corinthians 4:8–9

My cell is dark and deep,
Walls pressing in,
Crushing my bones.
How can light creep in here?
I've learned the secret of being content in all circumstances,
Says the letter-writer.
But what does that mean for me?
Courage,
Goes the whisper.
I'm disappointed, I scream back.
Pound my fists,
Cry my pain.
Courage,
Goes the whisper,
And there is the fissure
Where the light blinks
Then blazes.

5. COURAGEOUS WAITING

I arrive at the appointment half an hour early, just in case I can go in sooner than expected. I'm full of optimism. This will be the one day when things are running ahead of time. I won't be here all morning. I'm not very keen on waiting rooms.

An hour later, I'm slumped in the metallic chair, scrolling through my Facebook feed and tapping my feet. An announcement comes through from the reception desk: 'Clinic is running approximately an hour late today. We're sorry for the inconvenience.'

I sigh a bit, and settle back down. Should have brought a good book. My phone battery is dying – going, going, gone. I stare round at the four walls, letting my irritation mount.

Two hours in, and I've scoured the ragged magazines left on the table, even the two-year-old copy of *Take a Break*. I've learned some great tips for getting stains out of carpets and all about Victoria Beckham's beauty secrets, but I've taken none of it in, because I've been too busy stressing about waiting.

By the time I see the doctor, I'm anxious and fidgety and forget everything I was going to ask. I've allowed the waiting room to be a drain on me, wishing away the hours instead of seizing hold of the precious time I had.

The waiting time has become one huge vexation.

What are we waiting for?

Most of us are waiting for something.

Grace waits for Christmas with wide eyes and an expectant heart. Ben waits for exam results with guarded optimism and great anxiety. Daily we wait for buses and trains, and we spend a serious chunk of our lives waiting in queues. Our days are a series of waits, short or long.

Or perhaps we are waiting for something long term. To have a child, find a partner or recover from an illness. Sometimes we find that we are waiting all our lives for something that never happens.

Waiting is exasperating in a society where so many things are at our fingertips. When we want something, we click on an icon and have it at our front door within twenty-four hours. We download films and TV programmes and view them instantly, binge-watching those Netflix box-sets with no need to wait for the next episode. When I was growing up, I loved the feeling of anticipation while waiting for a camera film to be developed, not knowing how well my photos would turn out. The reality would usually be painfully bad, but the waiting was a heady time. Now they are right on a screen in front of me.

Computer scientist Ramesh Sitaraman has found that users of the internet manage patience for an average of only two seconds while waiting for a video or page to load online. A few more seconds, and we click away from the page, turning to something else for our entertainment.[1]

We have forgotten how to wait, in a world that values immediacy. Because of this, we find it more difficult when forced to wait, particularly when we are waiting for something which we think will make us happier. We think that we can't be at peace until that thing has come to fruition. We ask for answers right now, treating prayer like an app we can tap for immediate satisfaction, and we become discontented when our prayers seem to be unanswered.

We forget to search for God's work in our lives, *in* the waiting.

Waiting is painful. Nobody wants to wait, because waiting means delaying something that might be good. Sometimes the last thing we feel like doing is to accept the waiting, because that might even prolong it. It might mean we have to learn to trust the waiting, instead of ushering in the end of the waiting.

The Bible has a surprising amount to say about waiting. So many characters had to wait, some for many, many years. Abraham and Sarah waited for a promise to be fulfilled, a son given to them at an impossibly old age. Moses waited years in the desert before God called him to free the Israelites from captivity in Egypt. Hannah waited for a desperately longed-for child for many years before God gave her Samuel. The prophets waited for a time when God would restore Israel – many of them waiting all their lives. And Paul waited through much of his ministry in hardship, persecution and imprisonment.

If we look carefully at what it means to wait in these biblical accounts, we find one glaring truth: waiting is not sleeping; waiting is active.

But what does that mean?

Into the great unknown

Contentment. When the thing we are waiting for has arrived. When we are healed, or have more money, or feel more confident in ourselves. Contentment is something that happens to us, rather than something we chase and catch. It is happiness.

Really?

The word 'happy' is from the same root as the word 'happenstance' – which means a chance circumstance that usually produces a good result. In other words, we are happy when luck favours us, when the stars are aligned – when happenstances happen.

Not when we are waiting.

On the other hand, we might approach contentment as a more active decision to be satisfied with what we have. If we accept and are appreciative of it, we will be much happier – a 'count-your-blessings' mindset. This flies in the face of consumerism, which beats us up with the message that the more we have, the happier we will be.

But is it enough?

'I have learned the secret of being content in any and every situation,' (Philippians 4:12) Paul wrote from his prison cell, surrounded by armed guards, most likely under threat of execution. Paul didn't buy into the worldly wisdom of 'count your blessings', because he had very little to count. When we talk about counting our blessings, we are usually saying that we should look at the good things in our lives, whether they are relationships, a great career or material objects, and we should remind ourselves of them and be grateful for them.

This kind of gratitude is healthy for our souls. Paul often reminds us to be thankful. But what if we can't find much to count? What if we have been waiting for something for years? How would we then translate the advice to be content with what we have?

Paul never gave an easy set of answers, or ten steps to contentment. He never told his readers that they should 'just be happy', that, as a result of following Jesus, contentment would fall on us like soft rain or a warm blanket on a cold day. I'm so grateful he didn't, because I've learned something from my own long years of waiting: we can go beyond the need for answers, and discover something more profound. A God who understands, who has been through the most hideous suffering, who stoops to uphold the weak.

A God who turns the world's wisdom on its head.

Paul didn't provide us with solutions to the problem of suffering or the agony of waiting. Instead, he gave us a pattern of life, guidance for putting Christ first which results in a contentment way beyond the happiness we might feel when something great happens to us, and holds us through times of deepest darkness as much as through times of glittering light.

The first thing that Paul says about contentment is that he has *learned* it. He has made a decision to hold out his hands – and then follow through with his whole body, mind and spirit.

Contentment, therefore, is an *active choice*. It's a decision to live with the realization that we don't just sit back and receive peace because of circumstances, but we chase it through surrender to Jesus, knowing that it is only in him that true soul-rest can be found.

Active waiting allows us to sink deeper into God's embrace and into the great unknown of the mystery of grace.

Active courage in the waiting

Two characters who appear briefly at the beginning of Luke's account of Jesus' life give us an example of courageous waiting. First, we're introduced to Simeon (Luke 2:25), a 'righteous and devout' man. His name is translated as 'God has heard', and his life is a demonstration of this. We're told that he has been waiting for the promised Messiah who will come and comfort Israel. We don't know how long he has been waiting, but we get the impression that it's been a long time, because when Simeon takes Jesus in his arms, he cries out that now he can go in peace, because he has seen with his own eyes the salvation of all people – Gentiles (non-Jews) as well as Jews. His years of waiting have culminated in a shout of joy.

In his waiting, Simeon is full of the Holy Spirit. He chooses a life dedicated to seeking God's face, and the Holy Spirit reveals to him that he will not die before he sees the Christ. Simeon is called by God to wait, and so he waits, and when he sees Jesus, he knows immediately that his wait is over.

The second person we meet in this passage is a woman called Anna (Luke 2:36), which means 'grace'. Anna is named as a prophetess – a position of high calling – to speak God's words to others. Anna is at least eighty-four, and has been waiting for many years. Widowed only seven years into her marriage, she has been worshipping day and night in the temple all those years since. Anna could so easily have allowed her tragic situation to turn her to bitterness and discontentment, but instead she chooses to wait with active hope. She has been fasting and praying for the restoration of her people for so long, holding in her heart the hope that God will send a redeemer to come and bring peace to Israel, waiting quietly for God to bring answers.

Until now. Until two young parents bring a baby to be presented in the temple. Anna sees something in this baby which explodes joy deep in her soul, and she is full of thanks, going on to tell everyone she meets about the child who will restore lives and redeem Israel, fulfilling her calling as a prophetess in a fresh and vital way.

I wonder how Simeon and Anna felt in their waiting. I wonder if they cried out to God, asking *why*. Perhaps they sometimes clung on by a mere thread to the truth of the words they so loved, waiting and hoping, and sometimes waiting with little hope left.

What strikes me about both Simeon and Anna is their faithfulness. Both of them made a resolute decision to trust in God's saving work, even when the evidence could not be seen. They lived with a yearning expectancy, waiting and watching with the same kind of wonder as a small child waiting for Christmas – the Greek term used for Simeon's 'waiting for the consolation of Israel' in verse 25 translates as something close to 'waiting with hope' or, as Max Lucado puts it, 'waiting forwardly'.[2]

They didn't have to wait until they saw Jesus to meet with God, because both of them had learned a secret about who God was and what he was doing through their wilderness years. They experienced God waiting alongside them, and so trusted the waiting.

God's response to their faithful waiting was to shower joy on them in a holy moment. In those few minutes with that baby, their long wait was rewarded with an exhilarating, intoxicating answer to everything they had hoped for.

Open-ended waiting

What are you waiting for?

Henri Nouwen describes waiting as something that is open-ended. So much of our waiting is closed – we wait for something to change: the weather, our bodies, our circumstances. We want things to go in the direction we hope for, and when they don't, we are disappointed. Open-ended waiting, though, 'is an enormously radical attitude towards life'.³ It's an attitude where we sit at peace with the moment, where we treat waiting like a treasure rather than the irritation I described earlier in that waiting room.

To follow the examples of Paul, Anna and Simeon in their respective open-ended waiting, we should look carefully at how they waited. In all cases, the marks of their waiting hope were prayer, worship, patience and expectation. To follow their example, we need to get serious about our own prayer, worship, patience and expectation. Do we spend enough time with God? Do we live through our own waiting with a sense of hope – do we 'wait forwardly'?

What about you? What are you waiting for?

God longs to gather you in everlasting arms, to bind your wounds and tend your bruises, to wait with you. Heaven is waiting now, with bated breath, to restore all the earth and to bring you into the glorious freedom of knowing Jesus fully through eternity.

Yet the waiting can be so painful when times are raw, when we are totally broken. Can God reach out to us with contentment when we are shattered, waiting through the years to be made whole?

Prayer

Father,
When I am waiting,
Help me find the resources to say yes to you,
By the power of your Holy Spirit.
May I hold out my hands
And catch peace,
Even when storms pound the windows,
A peace which bundles up my pain
And flings it far from my soul.

May I wait with yearning expectancy
For a time when you will come
With invigorating vitality,
Drawing me into dreamed-for hope.
Help me take active courage
And learn contentment.
Amen.

Reflection

- Are you waiting for contentment with a sense of frustration at having to wait so long, through so much? What are you waiting for?
- What do you think about the idea that waiting can be a time of growth with God, and that in the waiting you might actually find that contentment you've been searching for?
- Reflect on Simeon's and Anna's stories in Luke 2. What strikes you about their responses to Jesus, and how will that help you in your waiting?
- You might want to read Tanya Marlow's *Those Who Wait* (Malcolm Down, 2017), a wonderful book which explores, through the lives of four biblical characters, the reality of waiting.

6. COURAGEOUS BROKENNESS

I watch the line of people waiting by the stage, shining faces wreathed in smiles. Waiting to tell us all about God's miraculous work of healing in their lives. 'God has healed my bad back,' a woman says, stretching out her arms. 'I feel great!' A man dances up and down and shouts excitedly about healed knees, and the gathered thousands whoop and cheer.

I shrink a little bit inside, fighting to balance my own sense of disappointment and my longing to rejoice with them. It's a bitter-sweet moment. There's a sense of frantic striving, trying to reconcile God's goodness with my un-healedness. How can I be filled up with all it means to be in God's grace if I am not healed? If I were healed, if I were whole, not broken any more, I would be more useful to God.

And the little voice inside asks, 'Why them, and not me?'

You just need to have faith

If we are broken, we are not exercising enough faith in our lives.

So I've heard them say.

Some teaching is emphatic about healing, wholeness and suffering, insistent that we're not supposed to be in pieces. We're meant to be fully whole – in body, mind and spirit.

At a large Christian gathering I considered going home early, because my condition was worsening by the minute. The pain was pressing in, an iron band snaking around my chest, and the coughing had started, indicating an infection taking root. Despite all this, I talked myself into going to the meeting that evening, because I felt the praise element would do me good.

I should have gone home.

After the talk, people were encouraged to pray for healing for those around them. I sat down in my chair, head in hands. I didn't want to be prayed for, not again, not tonight please. I had been prayed for so many times, both by trusted friends and by strangers. I simply didn't have the energy to face this again, to see expectant faces followed by disappointment. In an ironic way, it hurt too much to ask for someone to pray for the pain.

There are times when it's just too raw. But God is with us just as much when we sit with our head in our hands, exhausted and broken, as when we are full of faith and anticipation.

So there I was, soaking in God's presence, all I needed at that moment, when a man marched up to me and bellowed at me, really bellowed, 'God has called me to pray for you. What's wrong with you?'

If I had been feeling strong in body, I might have said thanks but no thanks and asked him why he was shouting in my face. Instead, I sighed inwardly and wondered if in fact God had sent him and I was being ungrateful. I muttered something about lung disease. 'God wants to heal you,' he said. 'To make you whole. Do you have faith that he will?'

I breathed in, pain stabbing all down my right-hand side. 'I . . . I never lose hope,' I managed.

He shot me a puzzled look and leaned in even closer. 'Just have faith,' he said, and clamped his hands on my pounding head with too much force. He prayed loudly, commanding the disease to be gone, practically ordering Jesus to take it away. As he said the words, the pain seemed to increase, radiating through my chest and over my shoulder blades. I was starting to feel stressed. He kept on praying, and I wanted him to stop. But in my sickness I felt too weak.

After a few minutes he stopped. I opened one eye discreetly. 'Well?' he said. 'Are you better?'

'Um . . .' I said, stammering. 'Well, I am still in pain.' Nothing if not truthful . . .

I saw his face fall. Physically.

Then he walked away. That was it. No acknowledgment of suffering, no praying for God to be with me. It seemed that I was a let-down. Not worth sticking with. No easy results here.

It felt like it was my fault.

Before this man prayed, I had been practising contentment in God's presence. The man's overbearing assurance that God wanted to make me whole cracked my courage and leaked in, and his response to my failure shattered it. For a moment I believed I was letting God down, that I should indeed be pressing more for healing, because that's what God wants for me. My fragile peace was dashed on the rocks of despair.

For a moment I forgot about courageous contentment.

Many others have been even more crushed by similar incidents, especially sick and disabled people who sometimes appear to be 'targets' for this kind of forceful language. I'm so dispirited that fragile courage is cracked open and exposed on the altar of insistence that God does not allow brokenness. How sad!

God, in his most wonderful inversion of this black-and-white thinking, is fully present *in* our brokenness rather than absent because of it.

A river of love

Another evening, another large gathering. This time, while still feeling poorly, I felt that little push from God to go to ask for prayer. I resisted for a time. I didn't really want to go through the whole rigmarole yet again and be faced with the inevitable discouragement. But the push got a little stronger, until it was more like a shove. 'OK, God,' I hissed, sounding like my teenage daughter. 'Whatever.'

This time God turned my somewhat bitter expectations on their head. A lovely woman came to pray with me, and didn't even ask me what was wrong. She said that she wasn't going to pray for physical healing for me, but was going to pray instead that I would encounter God.

And there and then, as she laid her hands on my head, so very gently with the softest of touches, I felt the presence of God flow through me, an enthralling river of pure, unadulterated love, like nothing else I'd ever experienced. From head to toe, like electricity, like power, but grace-filled power. And that was where I found my healing, my wholeness, all that I needed. My contentment.

If only this happened each time I was prayed for, if only I was able to tell the praying person of such a 'result'. I'm always such a people pleaser – I never want anyone to be disappointed in me! And yet, this is where some of us struggle: are we looking for immediate results of our prayers, or are we trusting God for something more long term and even more profound? Because God could well be working through the nothing and the misery and the silence. And we may never know how and why. But it does come down to the question, for both the praying person and the person being prayed for: do we trust in God? Whatever?

Broken works best

Author Catherine Campbell believes that God is in the brokenness as much as in the wholeness. When I read her story in *Broken Works Best*, I was overwhelmed by her faith-filled courage under the most appalling of circumstances. Catherine gave birth to three children, two of whom were profoundly disabled with life-limiting diseases. The girls, Cheryl and Joy, died at ten and thirteen years old. Catherine writes of a depth of experience of God's provision and peace in the storm, without excuse for the dark reality of the pain she lives with. She describes the harrowing moment when she found out that Cheryl was devastatingly ill, and how it made no sense to her: something must have gone badly wrong. She knew and loved God, so why didn't he protect her?

> Why did God not come up with the goods when I needed Him? Where was the promised happy life now? Have I been struck down, struck out, judged, condemned, forgotten, or, worse still, ignored? . . . Why did He have to break my heart?[1]

Catherine writes about what she came to discover 'true contentment' to mean. It's not about collecting nice things, she says, but more to do with 'an attitude of heart, learnt through pain'.[2] It's an attitude that chooses to exercise that contentment, whatever our situation, because of what Jesus has done. Catherine's suffering actually multiplied the peace of God in her life. She would never have experienced the peace that transcends all understanding, she says, if this turmoil had not thrown itself at her:

> It was pain that birthed a peace in my life that was at times tangible . . . I doubt that I would have sought to know God in the way that I have if my life's experience had always been trouble free . . . it was pain that sent me to his word on more occasions than joy, enabling me to learn more about the wonderful character and plans of God.[3]

Catherine testifies that her understanding of God's compassion was increased by her experience and by the tears she shed, reminding us of God's promise to keep track of all our sorrows, to collect our tears in a bottle (Psalm 56:8, NLT). At times, she knew God closer to her than any other person, and through the stripping away of everything in her life, she learned to trust in God in a more extensive way than she had done previously. Her pain has also enabled her to see Jesus like never before, as a suffering Saviour, a man of sorrows who 'took up our pain and bore our suffering' (Isaiah 53:4). Seeing Jesus in this light, she knew she could trust him and he would take her burden, because he was the one who understood the absolute horror of her loss like no other. She discovered that the Lord was able to sustain her as she left her burden of pain and sorrow at his feet.

This remarkable woman believes that if we allow God to take our broken lives, he can use them in astonishing ways. She wonders if we are missing out by thinking we have to be whole in every way to serve God, believing that whole is 'best'.

The glorious mystery of the now and the not yet

Sometimes we see windows into heaven.

We catch glimpses of God's kingdom working here on

earth, miracles of healing and transformation. We see people coming to Christ and being set free from bondage to addiction, or liberated from the pain of their past.

But at other times, we don't. It's like the windows are sealed shut, the hatches battened down.

Sometimes it's taught or implied in our churches that if we are not seeing remarkable things in our lives – if we are not being made 'whole' – we are getting it wrong. Healing brings wholeness in body and mind, and wholeness is what we are meant to have as Christians, what Jesus intended. Right?

Of course. Jesus travelled around bringing healing to many, and instructed us to do the same. When talking to the Pharisees about who he was and what he had come to do, Jesus did say that he had come to bring life in all its fullness (John 10:10). I firmly and fervently believe that God's design for us as dearly loved children is to know this fullness of life, and to come to a wholeness beyond our imaginings.

But what does wholeness mean?

In the first few chapters of his letter to the Romans, Paul has been exploring the idea that we are made righteous before God through faith, and now tells his readers how this works in practice in their lives:

> Therefore, since we have been justified through faith,
> we have peace with God through our Lord Jesus Christ,
> through whom we have gained access by faith into this
> grace in which we now stand. And we boast in the hope
> of the glory of God. Not only so, but we also glory in
> our sufferings, because we know that suffering produces
> perseverance; perseverance, character; and character, hope.
> And hope does not put us to shame, because God's love has

been poured out into our hearts through the Holy Spirit,
who has been given to us.

(Romans 5:1–5)

Paul digs deep into the rawness of human experience,
reminding us that God's design for our contentment never
meant to remove the experience of pain and sorrow, as if only
to bless the pain-free with the fullness of God's riches. This
passage speaks strongly to me of the 'now and the not yet'.
God's love is poured out on us, the hope of glory strong
within us, yet we live so often in suffering. Paul encourages
us to boast not in our own strength and togetherness, but
only in the hope of the glory of God. 'Hope' in this context
has been translated as something like 'happy certainty' –
something which isn't simply a glimmer on the horizon, but
a firm reality for those who take hold of it.

Paul then goes further: we should glory in our sufferings
because our suffering is achieving something. The *now*
we live in means we will suffer, through persecution and
simply through living in a broken world crying out for
freedom and redemption, but how beautifully Paul paints a
picture of us holding to the *not yet*, waiting in eager expectation for God to heal us, to make everything as it should
be. This hope – amidst the suffering – is where we catch our
contentment.

Taking God out of our pockets

The Bible never hints at an easy way out, or a respite for,
followers of God. Look at the Psalms: how many of them hint
at a level of pain and suffering we can barely comprehend?
Look at Job, the story of a man who lost everything, with
its startling lack of easy answers, its challenge to see God

differently, to take God out of our tiny pockets and search for a far bigger picture. Look at the prophets, who always inspired hope but also gave warnings and spoke of suffering as a part of life, like Isaiah:

> Do not fear, for I have redeemed you;
>   I have summoned you by name; you are mine.
> When you pass through the waters,
>   I will be with you,
> and when you pass through the rivers,
>   they will not sweep over you.
> When you walk through the fire,
>   you will not be burned;
>   the flames will not set you ablaze.
> (Isaiah 43:1–2)

This chapter is part of a section about God's promise to restore Israel from exile in Babylon. Isaiah is reminding the people of God's passionate love for them. They have been redeemed – they belong to the everlasting God. This is often used as a comforting passage, much as we discovered with the passage from Jeremiah. God has called us by name! We belong. The images of God walking with us through fire and raging rivers are incredibly powerful.

But I wonder if you've ever noticed the warning Isaiah is giving, as well as the encouragement. He is not saying that God will be with us *if* we go through difficulty, but *when* we go through difficulty. He is warning Israel that there are difficult times ahead. And the vivid picture language points to significant suffering – searing flames and turbulent water. 'The waves will not sweep over you' does not mean that you will be left unharmed, or that you will be rescued from a physical situation, but instead reminds you that because your resources are found in God's presence, you will withstand the roar of the rivers, for now and in eternity.

Personally, I find relief in that. God knows the difficulties we face in our lives. He knows it's a 'when', not an 'if'. He knows we are broken, but the good news is that he is here in the midst. This never gets old – the God who created the universe has redeemed you and called you by name, and is with you *through* the storm and the chaos.

I wonder if we have been deceived by a watered-down version of the gospel which refuses to face reality and chooses to make ourselves as comfortable as possible? And then, when bad things happen, it is no match for our distress and pain. Are we missing the glorious gospel Paul spoke of, a gospel fulfilled and sometimes deepened through suffering? Have we softened the truth of what Jesus accomplished so that we can be complacent consumers of a comfortable Christianity?

Fullness in frailty

We can reach out for contentment in our broken state. More than that, we experience a fullness of life that transcends and is mysteriously deepened by our pain.

Paul's theology about weakness is revolutionary. God partners with us within our imperfections, rather than waiting for us to be perfect, whole and completely sanctified. Paul's notion of God working in and through weak people doesn't tell us that the answers lie within ourselves, or that we are strong and victorious in everything, but that God values us and strengthens us in our weakness: 'But he said to me, "My grace is sufficient for you, for my power is made perfect in weakness." Therefore I will boast all the more gladly about my weaknesses, so that Christ's power may rest on me' (2 Corinthians 12:9).

Paul was addressing a specific situation in his life: his 'thorn', which may have been a physical illness. He'd begged God to take it away, but God hadn't done. Instead, God turned it right around, telling Paul that grace was enough. In a radical movement away from the 'wholeness is best' mindset, God shattered the values of the world, and in so doing, held out his version of contentment to weak people – to all of us.

We have a God who values and works through the weak. Jesus is the greatest example of this, being born into weakness and poverty, and dying on a cross, stretched out in stark vulnerability, yet achieving the greatest triumph in all history. Weakness is reflected throughout the Bible in the people God chose to partner with to bring the kingdom closer to earth. People like Moses, who had no oratory skills and may well have spoken with a stammer – in fact, he needed his brother Aaron to act as a mouthpiece for him. Gideon, the youngest and weakest of the most insignificant family, who couldn't believe that God would choose *him* and had to keep checking. David, the young shepherd boy who slew a giant, then messed up in spectacular fashion when he was king, committing adultery and bumping off his lover's husband. Mary, a young Judean girl with nothing particular to offer, unmarried, insignificant, but obedient. God works through weak people, and he works through people who are suffering.

God works with and through *you*.

Courageous contentment doesn't anticipate or expect perfection. It lives with a measure of frailty and weakness. It accepts that we may be broken, and does not expect that we wait to be mended before we can hope. The dazzling hope of the gospel is that we are, in fact, whole, because we hold to this life of steadfast hope.

Sometimes, though, the long-term disappointment at being broken is just too crushing. What do we do then?

Prayer

Lord,
When I don't understand why you don't act,
When I shrink a little inside,
When I can't hear your voice,
Will you sit beside me,
Will you abide with me,
Everlasting arms catching me?
Where I am frail, be my fullness.
Where I am weak, be my strength,
And where I am broken, be my restoration.
My courage in the rushing waters,
My contentment in the raging fire.
Amen.

Reflection

- How does the idea of the 'now and the not yet' speak to you?
- God didn't take away Paul's pain. 'Three times I pleaded with the Lord,' he wrote, 'to take it away from me' (2 Corinthians 12:8). Does this resonate with you?
- Reflect for a while on the passage about God's power in weakness from 2 Corinthians 12:7–10. What does this mean to you?

7. COURAGEOUS DISAPPOINTMENT

My writer friend Tanya Marlow has suffered from the chronic neurological condition myalgic encephalomyelitis (ME) for a number of years.

'In 2010, I gained a baby, and lost the ability to walk more than twenty metres,' she writes.[1] At the time of writing, there is no definitive cure for ME. Tanya describes it as feeling as if you are always trying to recover from a nasty flu strain. When she first became ill, she turned to God, but very reluctantly – 'Stomping, slamming the door, railing at him in my prayers. I was so very disappointed, and unable to understand why God had taken so much from me.'[2]

In *Coming Back to God When You Feel Empty* she explores the Old Testament book of Ruth, with a particular emphasis on Naomi and how she dealt with her desperate situation. Tanya weaves the story of these two women into her own story of suffering.

A space for stomping

In the time of the Judges who ruled over the two nations of Israel and Judah, Naomi, her husband and two sons left

Bethlehem during a famine. They moved to Moab, a land of pagans who hated her nation of Judah and worshipped a number of gods, sometimes making sacrifices of their children.

Naomi's family settled there, and her sons married local women, but within ten years her husband and both her sons had died.

Tanya relates her own feelings of bitter disappointment about an illness which has narrowed her life to the way Naomi must have felt after her loss. Naomi travelled back to Bethlehem, empty and bitter. 'I went away full, but the LORD has brought me back empty,' she told the people of her homeland, voicing her disappointment out loud, and calling herself 'Mara', which translates as 'bitter' (Ruth 1:21).

Tanya writes about how this account of Naomi shows us there is space for 'disappointment and stomping'. God is big enough – and loving enough – to take the bitterness we sometimes need to offload. Some people, Tanya says, including herself, need such an outlet; they need to 'stomp' at God, to shout, to cry and rally:

> So what do you do when God has taken, and you're left with nothing? Naomi stomps; Ruth clings. I do not wish to condemn those who respond like Naomi and me, who are overcome with bitterness. I love her honesty, and the fact that the Bible records her honesty with such tenderness.[3]

But, she says, however much God can take any venom we fling, there is something to be learned from Ruth's response to the situation. Ruth is such an interesting character because she makes a commitment to Naomi which will bring her nothing but sadness – or so it seems. She's just been through the loss of her husband, yet she vows to leave her homeland and wider family in Moab, and travel to her mother-in-law's homeland, a place despised by so many of her people. She responds with grace-filled determination, a desire to please Naomi and a longing to subsume herself into Naomi's land, people and God. 'Your people will be my people and your God my God,' she says (verse 16). Naomi responds to her situation with bitter disappointment, while Ruth responds with a promise and a longing to stay with Naomi. Tanya says there is room for both:

> Perhaps, like me, you are learning, slowly, to respond like Ruth. You want to come to God simply because you crazy-love him; you want to step into foreign lands when you have nothing, simply because you know his character.[4]

Later on, Naomi's bitterness will turn into joy. Ruth's act of courage in accompanying her mother-in-law will lead to something quite remarkable. In her destitution, she falls on the mercy of rich landowner Boaz, who, rather than treating her with contempt, is 'crazily generous' towards her, ensuring she and Naomi have enough grain, rather than taking advantage of this young woman who, literally, throws herself at his feet. His 'heart beats with God's own love for the poor and the vulnerable'.[5] Because Boaz treats Ruth with honour, he changes the course of her life, Naomi's life – and our lives still today.

'No longer called Mara, the bitter one, Naomi ends her days, as her name suggests, pleasantly, with a wedding and a grandson.'[6] That grandson was named Obed. Obed, who had a son named Jesse, who had a son named David, who would one day become king of Israel. Even greater than that, the line of David would one day produce a baby named Jesus.

Ruth's act of courage resonated through history, and this is reflected in the fact that she is named in the genealogy of Jesus (Matthew 1), one of a handful of women to be named. A foreign woman who made a choice to commit to her Jewish mother-in-law is honoured for her pivotal place in God's crazily generous salvation narrative.

Naomi's bitterness was lifted from her because of God's grace working in her life in more ways than she could possibly have imagined. She saw her many prayers answered, prayers cried out in moments of agony and loss. What a legacy she left us: an example of a life of sorrow still turned towards her God, still flooded with prayer, then transformed to praise as God brought her blessing and joy.

Tanya encourages us to live a life like Naomi's, full of prayer, remembering God's work in us and in our circumstances, even when we don't see the joy. This has helped Tanya herself turn around her own sense of bitterness many times, while holding on to the reassuring truth that we are *allowed* to be disappointed by God.

Both Naomi and Ruth acted out of courage in their sorrow. I believe that there are three courageous acts we can practise within our disappointment, all of which honour our sadness while turning our hearts to contentment: remembrance, thanksgiving and lament.

Remembrance: a remedy for bitterness

Why, God? When will you turn up?

The Psalms often share a sense of disappointment in God. In Psalm 77 the writer cries out for help, asking God when he will be heard, in what appears to be a personal reflection rather than an observation about a national situation. He asks a series of questions of God, summing up in one paragraph his ever-increasing despair:

> Will the LORD reject for ever?
>> Will he never show his favour again?
> Has his unfailing love vanished for ever?
>> Has his promise failed for all time?
> Has God forgotten to be merciful?
>> Has he in anger withheld his compassion?
> (Psalm 77:7–9)

I imagine many of us can identify with some of these feelings. In our pain it can be difficult to see where God is. We find it hard to see beyond our hurt and our circumstances, so we ask these questions. We scream out our agony. We doubt God's promises and wonder what happened to his unfailing love. Has God let us down? Is he angry with us? Where is God in this mess?

But the great thing about God's Word is that it both gives us permission to express our dismay and offers suggestions about what to do with it. The author of this psalm makes a very active decision, having cried out his agony: he remembers.

> I will remember the deeds of the LORD;
>> yes, I will remember your miracles of long ago.
> I will consider all your works
>> and meditate on all your mighty deeds.
> (Psalm 77:11–12)

Making a choice to remember heaves the psalmist out of bitter, self-obsessed navel-gazing. It may not change his situation, but what it does do is change his perspective. Reminding himself of God's deeds without minimizing his own disappointment is a courageous choice.

Thanksgiving: a balm for anxiety

Even so, if the bitterness and disappointment spring from something ongoing, something that is with us all the time, it can seem impossible to overcome our disappointment – even when we remind ourselves of God's work in our lives – because we may be experiencing anxiety. Worry and anxiety can be closely connected to a sense of disappointment and discontentment in our lives.

The persecuted Christians in Philippi have been living with a whole lot of anxiety about their situation, and Paul offers advice:

> Do not be anxious about anything, but in every situation, by prayer and petition, with thanksgiving, present your requests to God. And the peace of God, which transcends all understanding, will guard your hearts and your minds in Christ Jesus.
> (Philippians 4:6–7)

Paul has been reminding the Philippians that God is near to them, and so their attitudes should reflect their joy in one who upholds and strengthens them, even when they are facing trouble and disappointment. Praising comes before asking, Paul says, and we mustn't forget to thank God for all he has done in our lives.

I sometimes forget the praise and thanksgiving and run headlong into the petition, telling God what he should be doing, even earnestly on my knees for others. But without the attitude of gratitude, my prayers are somehow that bit flatter, and I wait for the peace beyond understanding in vain. If I remember to start out with praise and thanksgiving, something shifts: prayer seems more dynamic, and I recognize why Paul applied this passage to anxiety, for with true thanksgiving, anxiety has no choice but to flee – or at least to get itself into perspective.

But how can we pray 'with thanksgiving' in the midst of a situation which necessitates nothing but bitterness and sorrow? How can the woman who has just lost her husband to cancer pray with thanksgiving? What does that even mean, in situations of stark suffering?

Courageous lament

On news footage from a war-torn country I watched a woman stretched out on the ground, her fists pounding the rubble-strewn earth as she wept over the body of her child.

I often think that certain cultures are closer to a healthy reaction to horrific events than our Western 'suck it up and get on with it' response. When we are in acute pain, whether physical, mental or spiritual, we need to rail and weep, bleed and groan.

We need lament.

Lament is a candid, heartfelt outpouring of our sadness, our mourning, our pain, our fear. Lament is an intense, immersive way of communicating with God. There is a great difference between grumbling against God for our situation and crying out on our knees in pain to God. One is unhealthy and self-perpetuating; the other is courageous and meaningful.

Lament is scattered through Scripture, from Habakkuk to the Psalms, from Jeremiah through to Job – and, of course, there is an entire book named after it. Lamentations is a short series of laments over the destruction of Jerusalem. It's a book of poetry, a string of wails against God. The Hebrew title of the book is fascinating: *Ekah*. The word *ekah* translates as something like 'How . . . !' This is so much more immediate, somehow, and something many of us will identify with. *How, God? How?*

Much of Job's response to a situation beyond what most of us could bear is lament, born not out of a formed theology about God's nature, but out of acute suffering. Job cries out *ekah* – How . . . ! – to God over and over again, lost in his grief, mourning his loved ones and all he has lost. Yet he never rejects God, even when he has shouted lament to the heavens. He proves to the enemy, Satan, that God is right: that believers will still worship God even when their lives have fallen headlong into a pit of anguish, even when they have ranted and raved against him in their despair and hopelessness. That gives us a model – our ranting is normal and healthy, but we still worship. We don't accuse God, or dishonour God. We still praise. We still hold on.

Lament is an important part of living in the hope and future of the *not yet* – it's not about wallowing in despair, but more about joining in with the groaning of creation, a groaning that is waiting for things to be made right, a sense of woundedness that underlies everything we are, a long, heavy sigh at our brokenness. We all live in the great story, longing for the author to bring about the ending that will bring justice and peace and happiness. Our lament is a prayer, crying, *Come on, God. Bring it on. Come, Lord Jesus. Come soon.* It's more than a cathartic rant, although it can indeed bring a sense of relief. It's wider than complaint. It's a soul-level craving that can come out in screaming to the hills.

We are not consumed

In the middle of the book of Lamentations, the author comes to the apex of his lament about how Jerusalem is so desolate and lost. He has seen the destruction of the city, and weeps over the Babylonian invasion leaving the streets empty and lonely, his raw emotion shrieking his sadness and regret. He knows that it is the actions of the people of Jerusalem – their outright rebellion against God – which has brought them to this. Yet in the midst of his agony, he calls on hope:

> Because of the LORD's great love we are not consumed,
>   for his compassions never fail.
> They are new every morning;
>   great is your faithfulness.
> I say to myself, 'The LORD is my portion;
>   therefore I will wait for him.'
> (Lamentations 3:22–24)

We may be crushed, we may be disappointed, we may be uncomprehending, but we are not overwhelmed, because God's compassions never fail, and God's faithfulness is great. We may have come to this place of lament through our own sin, just as the people of Israel did, and need to take hold of God's forgiveness through the painful awareness of our own rebellion – but we are not consumed. We may have come to it because of living in a broken world, because of sickness or grief, depression or loneliness, unemployment or relationship breakdown – yet we are not consumed.

One day there will be no more lament, because there will be no more tears, no more mourning, no more death and no more agony. But for now, if you are in a place of lament deeper than disappointment and more painful even than hopelessness, if you are in a place where all you can do is scream, then scream. Scream and wail and pound your fists into God's chest, for God stands there as your Father who loves you more than anything you can imagine. God can take your anguish – there is a world of difference between asking pain-soaked questions in your desperate agony and charging God with wrongdoing.

God stands there and takes your hits and your questions and your shrieks of *why*, and then catches you up in an embrace which soothes and revives, which transforms mourning into dancing. No tear you cry is ever forgotten in the immense and endless love of your Father God.

Perhaps you are in a place where you are supporting others who need to lament, and your words of comfort and permission to lament to God in their disappointment will be what they need to hear. They do not need to put on a mask of being 'fine' around other Christians, because being authentic in their pain moves them closer to the Father's heart of compassion and liberation.

Let's encourage one another to be real, before God and before others. Don't berate yourself – or others – for disappointment. Don't hoard guilt for that shout-out at God. Dare to face your disappointment, and plunge yourself further into God's grace, held tightly in his arms.

Prayer

> Father,
> Sometimes I am so disappointed,
> And I don't understand why you haven't
>   changed things.
> Where are you?
> Have you forgotten about me?

Have you rejected me, or are you angry with me?
Has your promise failed for all time?
Hold me in my bitterness,
When I am Naomi,
And I weep.
Help me to remember you,
To recall your works of power in my life,
To remind myself of the way you have saved me, and
Your overflowing, generous grace,
Your heart of outrageous compassion.
Amen.

Reflection

- In what ways are you, or have you been, disappointed with God?
- Do you identify more with Ruth or Naomi in the way they respond to their situation? Do you think there is something to be learned from the other way of responding? How could that help you?
- What do you think about the three things we explored which may help in times of disappointment – remembrance, thanksgiving and lament? Do any of these resonate with you at this time?
- Think about what you are disappointed with, and spend some time giving these things to God, reflecting on the passage from Lamentations 3.
- If you are in a time when you need to lament, read through some of the psalms and find one that expresses what you want to say. Spend some time using the words to talk to God about your pain.

8. COURAGEOUS PERSEVERANCE

My daughter was two-thirds of the way round a very muddy 2 km cross-country course in driving rain and poor visibility.

But something was odd. I couldn't see her in the crowd of runners. I strained to see through the pelting rain, and spotted a lone figure with a bedraggled blonde ponytail squatted down behind the main body of runners. She seemed to be fiddling with her trainer. She looked up, saw the last of the runners struggle past her, shrugged her shoulders and followed on, limping. It was only at the end of the race, when she'd dragged herself last across the finishing line with a smile on her face, that we realized what had happened. One of her trainers was now embedded deep in cloggy Shropshire mud, but instead of giving up and sinking to the ground in defeat, she'd left it there and kept going, one shoe off, one shoe on.

We threw away those socks.

Perseverance is paddling

Courageous contentment is all about perseverance.

Reepicheep, the small but valiant Narnian talking mouse

from *The Voyage of the Dawn Treader*, knows something about perseverance. When his ship arrives at an island after many months of struggle through the ocean, many of the crew don't want to carry on. They've had enough. They want to turn back, because what might be ahead makes them too fearful.

But Reepicheep has been given a promise. He's been told that one day he will find the 'utter east', and not to doubt or turn back. There he will find all he is searching for. Aslan has sparked something in his deepest being, and he is ready to go for it with all his might:

> While I can, I sail east in the *Dawn Treader*. When she fails
> me, I paddle east in my coracle. When she sinks, I shall swim
> east with my four paws. And when I can swim no longer,
> if I have not reached Aslan's country, or shot over the edge
> of the world in some vast cataract, I shall sink with my nose
> to the sunrise.[1]

Reepicheep is living with a goal in sight. Whatever happens to him, he will never turn his face away from his sure and certain future. He will paddle in pursuit of Aslan's country until his coracle fails, and then swim until he can swim no longer, always looking upwards.

Even when he is sinking.

Beautifully overshadowed

Contentment is not perseverance, though, is it?

Contentment is a cat, sleeping curled up by a roaring fire, or someone lying on a beach, basking in the sunshine. Laid-back satisfaction. The world can stop; there is nothing to do. One synonym of 'contentment' in thesaurus.com is 'complacency'. Most of the other synonyms indicate something similar: satisfaction, repletion, fulfilment, gratification, equanimity.

But as we know by now, Paul's idea of holy contentment isn't like the world's notion of contentment. In Paul's thesaurus, contentment is all about setting Christ first, and so the most contented follower of Christ is the one who will never be complacent. She's the one who will be pressing on to know Christ and be more like him:

> Not that I have already obtained all this, or have already
> arrived at my goal, but I press on to take hold of that for
> which Christ Jesus took hold of me. Brothers and sisters,
> I do not consider myself yet to have taken hold of it.
> But one thing I do: forgetting what is behind and straining
> towards what is ahead, I press on towards the goal to win
> the prize for which God has called me heavenwards in
> Christ Jesus.
> (Philippians 3:12–14)

Paul knows he is complete in Christ, and has already been claimed by Christ, but he has not yet obtained the fullness of knowing Christ (verses 10–11). He knows there is more to come, and that it's up to him to take hold of it. In the verses preceding this passage he has been talking about the 'surpassing worth' of knowing Christ Jesus. He considers everything he had before – all the things he took pride in, such as his learning and zeal for religion – to be nothing compared to gaining Jesus. Instead of his own righteousness making him important, it's now his faith in Christ making him far less important but far more perfectly whole in being part of God's family. This has become all he wants and all he needs: to know more of Christ and to live in the power of the resurrection.

Paul uses the language of being completely taken over by Christ, like wings spread over us. 'Christ Jesus took hold of me' is translated in the Greek as something like 'overtaken' or even 'overwhelmed'. We need have no fear; we are beautifully overshadowed. How glorious!

Paul then uses this expressive picture to springboard his urge to persevere. We are most contented when we are not 'satisfied' with our progress in following Christ and taking his Word to others. His encouragement to press on is about taking ourselves above this kind of self-satisfied state and increasing our drive to be more like him. The more passionately we pursue Jesus, the more we are centred on him and at peace in him.

Paul's emphasis in the next chapter of Philippians is about rejoicing in all circumstances, learning contentment and knowing the peace God gives which is beyond comprehension. All these proceed from this sense of being utterly overtaken by God and pressing on to know him more.

But how do we press on towards this goal?

Pressing on is forgetting

Kate[2] had been into some shocking stuff in her past. She'd got involved with a local group who practised witchcraft, and they had taken delight in cursing the churches nearby and leaving symbolic items for them to find. Kate became a Christian when a friend took her to church. She thought she would be rejected because of all the havoc, but instead she was welcomed with open arms and loved. She experienced the power of the Holy Spirit in a highly tangible rush of pure love, and turned her back on all she had been a part of.

She shared with me that it had been difficult. She'd been well regarded in the group, taking on the role of a priestess. She'd had a lot of power and had known a lot of satisfaction. In her first months and years as a Christian she would find herself almost pining for the person she had been and the feelings her position had given her, despite her decision to follow Jesus. As time went on, she became more and more immersed in Christ's love, and less and less steeped in the life she had known. She started to make a constant choice to put this darkness behind her: to forget it, to leave it where it was, and to push her whole being into knowing more of God and living in the way of Christ. While she never forgot her past, and some days had to struggle more than others, her perseverance led her closer and closer to Jesus, and she was transformed. She was utterly forgiven and set radically free from all she had been bound up in.

When Paul mentions his own past life of pride and his persecution of followers of Christ, he calls it rubbish compared to the reality of how he is living now. In pressing on, he lets go of what he used to be, which means letting go of the prestige of his former life as well as the memories of the kinds of things he did. He might well have felt torn by this, because he had known very high status.

Part of letting go is entering into God's pure and perfect forgiveness, and part of it is in choosing to keep it behind rather than with us. That doesn't mean that we literally forget about things in our past, but more that we will put them aside in order to go forward following Jesus. When we 'forget' – or choose to leave the things that bind us up so tightly behind us – we are in a good place to push forwards.

Are you ready to forget those things you have held on to in the past – things that hold you down, or things you need to repent of?

Pressing on is straining

A video that went viral on social media showed a primary school sports day where the year 6 boys held back and assisted a boy with disabilities across the finishing line, in such a way that he won the race. The boy made a massive effort on his own, straining towards that finishing line with all his might, but his mates gave him the impetus to finish and gain the prize.

'Strain' is an interesting word because it looks nothing like laid-back complacency. To strain towards something is to put our whole self into it, to be moving forward, often through something difficult or sticky.

Paul saw a great prize ahead. He knew that everything in him was made right – his spirit at inexpressible peace – when he was going for this prize with all his might. He wasn't striving for success in the eyes of others, or making himself do something impossible, but training himself to go for this soul-transforming reward with every particle of his being.

Much like Reepicheep in his coracle.

If we focus our minds on our eternal future, our citizenship in heaven, we will always be stretching ourselves towards that glittering prize. Not for our own glory and success, but because we long to follow Jesus, and live drenched in the dynamic power of being loved by God.

We can't do this race on our own. The little boy in the video got himself across the line with sheer grit and determination, but only with the help of the other lads. We have no less than the Holy Spirit to power us through, to increase our courage, to link arms with us and spur us on. We are not alone in our strivings, not isolated when we are pressing ahead with all our might, because God is here, arm in arm with us, holding us upright as we stumble across that line.

Pressing on is groaning

Paul groaned with pain and suffering.

His determination to go for the prize was fuelled by his certainty that he belonged to Jesus, but it was also tested in many situations, not least when he repeatedly pleaded with God to take away his 'thorn'. Yet he knew that this present time of pain couldn't be compared to the prize that he would one day win:

> I consider that our present sufferings are not worth
> comparing with the glory that will be revealed in us.
> For the creation waits in eager expectation for the children
> of God to be revealed . . . We know that the whole creation
> has been groaning as in the pains of childbirth right up
> to the present time. Not only so, but we ourselves, who
> have the firstfruits of the Spirit, groan inwardly as we wait
> eagerly for our adoption to sonship, the redemption of our
> bodies.
> (Romans 8:18–19, 22–23)

Paul had been reminding the Christians in Rome that they were no longer condemned. The work of Christ and the power and presence of the Holy Spirit in them offered abundant life and peace, testifying in their spirits that they were God's children. He then went on to give this message of hope – and longing – about their future.

I've always found this a powerful passage which reflects the depth of reality many of us face in our own anguish. We are waiting with pain and with hope, and the only way we can express this is in groans too deep for words. Creation itself groans with us, resonating with our inward groans of pain and sorrow. We are God's children and heirs, and so for now we share in God's sufferings – we live in brokenness, eagerly awaiting the redemption of our bodies.

God didn't take away Paul's thorn, and God didn't take away Jesus' pain on the cross, the most starkly intense pain that any human being could possibly experience – not only the physical wounds of crucifixion, but the spiritual wounds of sin of every single human person who ever lived and ever will live. His suffering was heavy with sheer anguish and heartache and misery and pain and weeping and wretchedness. Even more agonizingly, he felt forsaken and wrenched from his experience of the Father's presence. Unimaginable.

God doesn't always take away our pain. But what we live through cannot compare with the glory that will be revealed in us. We live balanced on a knife-edged ambiguity of present suffering and hope indescribable – thank God for this glorious hope!

Pressing on to know Christ grants us a joy-filled release, a sense of hope that penetrates even the depths of darkness in which we find ourselves. That light shines into our darkest corners, shattering the gloom and exploding the shards of heaviness into dazzling brightness.

Our bodies may groan, our souls may weep, but we press on with courage. We press on knowing that what is before us is so much greater than what is behind. We persevere because all that we are responds to God's ongoing work in our lives, drawing us closer to himself and flooding us with extravagant joy.

May you be filled with courage as you read this. May you be courageous in your waiting and in your brokenness, in your disappointment and in your daily perseverance, sometimes dragging your feet when you lose your shoe in cloggy mud, sometimes skipping with energy. May you reach for the prize of being called heavenwards in Christ

Jesus, and live in contentment as you inch towards that finishing line.

Prayer

Father,
When I am caged in suffering and sorrow,
Give me the strength to choose to persevere,
To press on towards the prize of your glory,
Which breaks through the strongest of prison bars.
Give me power in my weakness to strive to the end,
Overwhelmed by your love,
Belonging to you.
May I learn a holy contentment
Which soars above my circumstances,
Which lifts up my head and my hands.
Thank you that your greater hope sustains me,
And never, ever lets me go.
Amen.

Reflection

- What goals are you pressing on towards? Are they glorifying to God? How do you know if they are?
- Reflect on Philippians 3:12–14. Think particularly about the words, 'Christ Jesus took hold of me', letting Jesus overwhelm and take hold of you now. What do these words mean for you?
- We're halfway through our exploration of contentment. What do you think about the word now – has its meaning changed for you at all?

PART 3:
CAPTIVATED CONTENTMENT

I will be satisfied as with the richest of foods;
with singing lips my mouth will praise you.
Psalm 63:5

Praise. Celebrate. Worship. Adore. Extol. Feast. Exalt.
Glorify. Rejoice. Party!
I'll say it again: rejoice! the writer says.
All day, every day.
Bask. Delight. Enjoy. Luxuriate. Relish. Savour.
Thrive. Wallow.
Revel!
Enchanted by glory,
Enthralled by yearning,
Satisfied by grace.
Even in darkness
I hold out my arms wide,
To catch something.
Something which pierces the murk,
Something breathtaking in power.
Something captivating.

9. CAPTIVATED BY WORSHIP

In my teenage years, I attended youth meetings run by the band Heartbeat at Kingdom Faith Camp. I will always remember one particular evening, because I experienced the glory of God in an amazing way.

It was towards the end of a praise and worship session. About five hundred fourteen-to-eighteen-year-olds were gathered in a big tent, discovering the adoration of God. Rain pounded on the roof, and so did the Holy Spirit. It wasn't sudden, more like a gradual realization, a stirring in my stomach, a lightness of spirit, an awareness of something happening.

My eyes were open, but something was pressing on them. I became aware of something that felt like a cloud spread across the ceiling, a cloud that covered the place, heavy and dark, yet alive with a sense of light and life. One by one, we fell on our knees, and then we fell prostrate, lying full out on the damp grass with our faces to the ground. For me, it felt like the cloud was falling over me, embracing me. It was like nothing I could ever describe.

It was glory, and it was absolutely captivating.

In the middle of a confusing time for me I discovered what it meant to be enthralled by God. Despite my struggles with self-esteem and bullying, my hatred of my sick body, something shifted. It would still be a long time before I experienced healing in my emotions, but God's glory touched me and changed me that holy night. God's glory set me on a new path, a path towards contentment.

The purpose of us

We're made for relationship, made for one another.

But we're made for something even more than this. A group of seventeenth-century theologians put it like this: 'The chief end of man is to glorify God by enjoying him forever.'[1] Glorifying God draws us to the deepest fulfilment any person could ever possibly find.

In his book about enjoying God, John Piper claims that when we are most satisfied in God, God is most glorified: 'His glory shines in your happiness, when your happiness is in him.'[2] This isn't about a pursuit of happiness for our own sake – it doesn't claim that God is most glorified when we are most satisfied, but only when we are most satisfied *in God*. When we chase headlong after God's glory rather than our own happiness, it results in a heightened state of contentment.

Because we are created for worship.

Why do we worship?

Someone posting on a forum about Christianity questioned the idea of worshipping God: 'Worship looks so boring. Why do you bother? Is it just because you have to? Isn't that a bit egotistical of God?'

When C. S. Lewis was an atheist, one of his main blocks to faith was all the commands to bring praise to God in the Psalms. It seemed to him that God was as desperate for our worship as a vain woman searching for compliments. He couldn't conceive of a God like that to whom he would actually want to give praise, because he saw such a God as self-serving and arrogant, a remote figure who wanted nothing from us but a kind of coddling, a massaging of a tender ego. How could a God like that even deserve worship, let alone claim to love us?

Later in his life, after his conversion, Lewis reflected on how he had felt about worship and glorifying God. He'd missed the point about praise, thinking of it only in terms of giving honour to something or someone, or complimenting someone. He'd never recognized that all enjoyment actually overflows into praise. In their invitations to praise the Lord, the psalmists were just doing what we all do when we talk about something we think is great.

Praising God later came to mean perfect contentment to him. Delighting in God brought his soul 'supreme beatitude': 'Drunk with, drowned in, dissolved by that delight . . . bliss . . . Fully to enjoy is to glorify. In commanding us to glorify Him, God is inviting us to enjoy Him.'³

C. S. Lewis's answer to his atheist self was to remind himself that worship and praise are not only an act of obedience, but that God also heaps riches on us when we worship. When we praise our children or a friend, we do not harbour resentment towards them. Instead, we often feel a warmth, something we may be bursting with, as the act of praise achieves something in our own spirits too.

Glorifying God can transport us to depths of delight and heights of rapture, and wash through our spirits like a deluge of rain. God loves our worship, rejoices in our joy, takes pleasure in our contentment. Our worship, out of a place of longing to honour God, releases freedom.

It's not easy for our me-centred culture to grasp that we become most whole when we are bringing praise to God. People kick out at the idea of worshipping God because it seems to undermine our own autonomy as human beings: why should we praise someone else? But they are missing the point: praise is as much made for us as it is for God. Praise is liberating and transformative. In praise I often find an alleviation of anxiety, a new perspective and a sense of peace I cannot comprehend. In praise my pain is gathered up and made less of, and all the more so when it is severe.

And sometimes I 'feel' none of those things – but God asks that I obey anyway, and I know that this is both what he requires of me and how he blesses me. (We'll be exploring those darker times further on in this section.)

So bringing glory to God and delighting in him draws us to freedom and satisfaction. But how should we worship?

From thundering organs to Hillsong

'Your church doesn't worship properly. I've been there. They don't have an organ or a choir. There's no sense of awe, you know?'

'Well, *my* church has it right. We have this great worship band and there's such a sense of intimacy with God. It's not all formal and stiff like yours.'

When I was younger, I was rather dogmatic about worship styles and which one was The Best. I was brought up on evangelical charismatic-style worship (within the constraints of the Church of England, so never reaching the most glorious of heights), and that was where my heart was. I went to the more charismatic festivals every year and revelled in the worship there; it was so *me*. I could be free to worship God there – and God always met with me. God *never* met with me in other more traditional forms of worship.

Or so I thought.

Could it be possible that I never gave God the chance?

I remained fairly stubborn about this until my husband was appointed to a curacy in a rather more traditional church than I would have preferred. I railed at God and at my long-suffering husband: how am I going to survive here? How am I going to be 'fed'? What about the kids? And yet, when I visited the church, organ and all, I had a sense that God was, in fact, calling us there, and I'd better like it or lump it. Somewhat sulkily, I said yes to God and yes to Tim, and prepared to put up with standing for the Gloria and singing the hymns, armed with a somewhat martyr-type attitude.

It wasn't very glorifying to God, really.

It was in one of the very first services that God spoke to me very clearly. I was singing the hymns, secretly planning where I could go to get 'properly fed', when I heard a still small voice: 'You are being a petulant child.' I was caught short, a little surprised. After all, I was only ensuring that the children and I would be able to keep strengthening our faith, that we would be able to go somewhere with a style that suited us. But no. God was very clear, deep in the reaches of my sullen heart. 'Do you really mean these words?'

I looked down at the hymn I was singing, a hymn I'd never heard before, and, as far as I was concerned, never wanted to hear again. But then I looked at the words. Really looked. Read words which spoke of praise, of loving God with my whole heart, of following him wherever he sent me, of delighting in him and praising him until the end of my days, and the reality hit me. I wasn't singing these words like I meant them. I was singing them like I was bored and couldn't be bothered. Like there was something better around the corner and I just had to put up with this while I waited.

And then I knew, as the Holy Spirit whispered words of life into my spirit, that if I really meant these words, then I needed to jolly well mean these words. Drop the attitude, drop the entitlement, drop the arrogance. In that moment God transformed my attitude, and I was different. I lost my haughty pride and my insistence that I couldn't be 'fed' in a place like this. And as I lost it, I encountered God in the depths of the worship that flowed from my repentance.

My natural taste hasn't changed, but my spirit has, and now, whenever I walk into a church, I am very careful not to think about what it can do for me. It's all about what I bring to God in that moment, about me making a sacrifice of praise, and deciding that I will worship with my mind, heart and strength, as God requires of me. Because of this, I have encountered God in Book of Common Prayer services, Taizé-style services, middle-of-the-road C of E services, high-up-the-candle healing services and meetings of a Chinese Fellowship (in Mandarin), among many others. This has widened my knowledge of, and love for, God, who is, after all, wider than any of us can ask or imagine. How was I ever so arrogant as to think that I could only encounter God in the way I wanted? I'm so grateful to God for opening my eyes and changing me from within. For sanctifying me.

Wired for worship

When we glorify God wherever we find ourselves, God meets us. If we don't think of church in terms of what we get from it, of how it feeds us, but instead in terms of what we are going to bring to it today, we will experience something so much more profound than the buzz of a song we like or a sermon that speaks to us. Something more like the unknown depths of the riches of who God is.

Glorifying God isn't just about church services and singing, though. We give God glory when we live our lives in obedience to his Word, when we love him and love others, as Jesus summed up in the commandments. The way we act in our daily lives, in all our messes and conflicts and pain and disappointments, can bring God glory – or not.

Contentment comes in putting ourselves – our own needs and desires and sense of entitlement – to death, looking at God and reflecting the glory of God. As we look more at him and allow ourselves to become entranced by his presence, we reflect his glory as we are transformed into his image. And it's in being conformed to that likeness that we end up closer to wholeness.

Glorifying God sets us free while bringing praise to the one we love, whether through contemporary worship songs in a warehouse or through quiet meditation on a sickbed. It doesn't matter where we praise or when we praise, but let's praise, because we are created to do so.

How are you going to bring glory to God today, where you are, however flawed this may be, however difficult for you?

True and proper worship

In Paul's letter to the Romans, he has been teaching the Christ-followers in Rome about their need for salvation and how to be saved. Now he turns to what it means to live out their new lives as Christians:

> Therefore, I urge you, brothers and sisters, in view of God's mercy, to offer your bodies as a living sacrifice, holy and

> pleasing to God – this is your true and proper worship. Do
> not conform to the pattern of this world, but be transformed
> by the renewing of your mind. Then you will be able to test
> and approve what God's will is – his good, pleasing and
> perfect will.
>
> (Romans 12:1–2)

When we offer ourselves to God as a living sacrifice, it is a transformative act, an act of the will in the renewal of our minds. In being made subject to Christ, we are deliberately stepping out in a decision to reject the pattern of this world, and in making that active decision, we are more able to hear what God is saying to us. Paul's idea of worship isn't caught up in what songs to sing, what prayers to say or who should do what in a service, but in where our minds are, and our own personal decision to follow God in this moment. Every time we choose not to conform to this world's enticing call, we are holding our arms out for more contentment in Christ, because we are allowing ourselves to be changed. Every decision to reject gossip or to be kinder to someone we disagree with or to care for someone in great need is a decision of true and proper worship, and each time we choose this attitude of heart, we are being made holy and pleasing to God.

Being captivated by God is about an attitude of submission, one that flies in the face of human cultural wisdom, puts ourselves under God, lifts him higher and says, *Yes, I will do as you ask*. 'True and proper worship' is not worship that springs from our own pride and self-satisfaction, but from laying ourselves down – and only in so doing can we catch that contentment that comes from being wholly, audaciously enchanted by God.

Freedom in drops of blood

Jesus himself modelled this kind of true and proper worship in its most perfect form, wrestling with his pain and fear on the Mount of Olives the night before his crucifixion: ' "Father, if you are willing, take this cup from me; yet not my will, but yours be done" . . . being in anguish, he prayed more earnestly, and his sweat was like drops of blood falling to the ground' (Luke 22:42, 44).

This picture expresses a pain so desperate, an anguish so starkly acute. I don't think we can even begin to imagine what it looked like, because it was so much more all-encompassing than anything we could ever experience. Jesus was taking on the unimaginable mountain of human sin in his body.

And yet he said yes, in an act of pure and perfect worship. He found the resources to do this on a night of staggering despair. He knew what was going to happen, knew that what lay ahead would be the most hideous experience that any human being would ever suffer. He knew that he would be crushed in every way: bodily, emotionally, physically and, perhaps most of all, spiritually. And yet he accepted. Accepted with sweat pouring from him, but still accepted.

Jesus' example is difficult to follow, but he showed us that in an attitude of true and proper worship he could reach out for all his Father had for him, as well as bring glory to his Father. Instead of boasting about who he was and demanding worship and acclaim, he quietly laid himself down and gave his whole self so that we might be free. He had a choice, and he made it.

I am so grateful. Aren't you?

We've thought about being captivated by worship, but what does that look like? Can we be satisfied in God, and is that really enough?

Prayer

Dear Jesus,
I give you glory and honour,
Bow before you in worship,
Lift you high as the Name above all names.
Thank you that you made me to praise you
And that in praising you, I find freedom.
Help me say yes to you,
Even on my nights of despair.
May my spirit respond to you
In perfect surrender,
Not waiting for answers.
Drench me in joy unspeakable
As I immerse and dissolve myself in you,
And catch holy contentment.
Amen.

Reflection

- How have you experienced the presence or the glory of God?
- What are your thoughts about worship?
- Meditate for a few moments on the words C. S. Lewis uses about this kind of authentic worship of God: 'drunk with, drowned in, dissolved by . . . bliss'.
- What is God saying to you about your own worship?
- Spend some time reflecting on Romans 12:1–2. Ask God to show you how you can present yourself as a living sacrifice, and have your mind transformed so that you are closer to a place of captivated contentment.

10. CAPTIVATED BY SATISFACTION

Three-year-old Lily Robinson looked at a loaf of tiger bread one day and decided that the pattern looked far more like a giraffe than a tiger, so she wrote to Sainsbury's supermarket to suggest they change the name: 'Why is tiger bread called tiger bread? It should be called giraffe bread. Love from Lily Robinson, aged 3½.'

Chris King, a customer service worker, wrote back to her, saying he thought that was a brilliant idea: 'It looks much more like the blotches on a giraffe than the stripes on a tiger, doesn't it?' He explained why tiger bread is called tiger bread: 'It is called tiger bread because the first baker who made it a looong time ago thought it looked stripy like a tiger. Maybe they were a bit silly.' He signed his name 'Chris King (age 27½)' and included a gift card for Lily to buy some tiger bread and some sweets.[1]

This worker went above and beyond to make a small child happy, and the nation responded by sharing the story multiple times on social media, the comments alight with more than a glow of satisfaction. 'Awww ... that's so lovely.' 'That worker shows what customer service should be.' 'The world doesn't feel so bad when you get people like that.'

Satisfaction is a warmth, a knowledge that all is right with the world after all, that things are OK. Satisfaction makes us feel safe, like we belong here, like we can let out a huge sigh of relief. Sainsbury's did a good job, because they did something they didn't have to do, and so engaged a desolate place in us: that place which is longing for unexpected joy.

The parts other satisfactions cannot reach

Do you remember the old Heineken advert? It made a lofty promise: it would refresh the parts other beers could not reach. The ad worked because it appealed to something in us all – a sense that our inner being craves a kind of satisfaction, and nothing quite hits the spot. People often speak of a yawning sense of emptiness, something that can never be filled, even when they live a life full of wonderful experiences and fulfilling relationships.

St Augustine said, 'You stir man to take pleasure in praising you, because you have made us for yourself, and our heart is restless until it rests in you.'[2] All the things we chase so hard don't give us this kind of heart-rest – only God can satisfy those fathomless parts of us, the broken pieces which may remain broken but are loved and tended by God's amazing grace. We saw earlier that there is something that happens in God's presence when we delight in God, when we immerse ourselves in God, which completely changes us, comprehensively shifts our outlook. It doesn't necessarily change the situation, but it can make all the difference to perspective. God means for us to find satisfaction – and joy – in our worship.

Scripture makes it clear that God will do more than satisfy; God will pour out, overflow, overwhelm, saturate us. We will be submersed in God's love until we can hardly bear it, be so mesmerized by God we won't be able to contain it.

Thousands of years before that Heineken ad, David made the same claim about God. He claimed that God gave him such a profound level of satisfaction – and it was captivating:

> Because your love is better than life,
>   my lips will glorify you.
> I will praise you as long as I live,
>   and in your name I will lift up my hands.
> I will be satisfied as with the richest of foods;
>   with singing lips my mouth will praise you.
> (Psalm 63:2–5)

David wrote this song at a disastrous time in his life. His son Absalom had instigated a mass rebellion against him, and David had fled to the desert, cut off from his beloved home and from God's presence in the temple, terrified and uncertain about what his future might hold. Nevertheless, he sat in the dryness of the wilderness and chose to praise God.

This isn't a song about feeling a bit better in God's presence, but about *bursting* with satisfaction, like after the most delicious meal. This is the kind of satisfaction that comes from spending a lot of time seeking God.

But this song is about something more, even, than satisfaction . . .

Springs of living water

She's walking to the well, hot and thirsty, when she sees him. A man. A Jewish man, at that. She tugs her head covering further over her face and shuffles by, dragging her feet in the dust, head bowed. If he notices her, he will walk away. Might even spit on the ground. She knows she's hated – a woman, and a Samaritan. The taboo of all taboos. Besides that, men reject her. Five times she's been dumped, left with nothing, and this time her man won't even give her the security of marriage. No. She's a nothing, discarded and detested.

But he turns to her. Speaks to her. Asks her for a drink. What is happening here? How can he do that? Surely, he knows that he'll be ceremonially unclean if he handles the same vessel as her? Surely, he knows she's utterly worthless? She stares at him, her heart thumping. Who is this man, with eyes that pierce her soul?

That's when he starts talking about living water, and her life changes beyond recognition.

In this irresistible, radical passage in the Gospel of John, Jesus isn't talking about physical water. He describes living water as a substance which means that we will never thirst again, 'a spring of water welling up to eternal life' (John 4:14). Something so far beyond physical sustenance – a form of nourishment that sustains our souls, cascading into our empty spaces. He addresses discontentment at its deepest level, saying that only he can assuage the void at the heart of us. The woman responds with longing, asking for this water. She recognizes something in Jesus, something she needs beyond water and life itself. She knows she is thirsty and that only he can satisfy that raging thirst, a thirst she perhaps hasn't even recognized before this moment. In Jesus, she encounters a man who subverts her experience of men. He doesn't reject her in her womanhood or her race or her sin, but instead speaks directly to the heart of who she is and gives her the very thing she needs most: water which satisfies beyond any satisfaction she could ever imagine. Later she tells everyone she knows about Jesus, unable to hold him in or keep this immense, life-giving power to herself. She is overwhelmed – and overflowing.

I hope it changed her for good, hope it captivated her and kept hold of her until she found contentment beyond words. I'm sure it did, for who could ever encounter Jesus and come away unchanged?

Full to overflowing

As we've already discovered, in the book of Romans Paul was encouraging the Christians in their new lives of discipleship. He had been urging them to greater unity, because his heart was for their liberation from the bondage of sin and for them to know freedom and delight in Christ. In the final verse of his formal teaching to the Roman Christians, he gathered up all his thoughts and prayers with some words about overflowing: 'May the God of hope fill you with all joy and peace as you trust in him, so that you may overflow with hope by the power of the Holy Spirit' (Romans 15:13).

When we fill our car tanks with petrol or diesel, we sometimes fill them to the brim if we're going on a long journey, but we can't fill them to overflowing. That would just be messy, and wasteful. But the power of the Spirit doesn't work like that. In God's economy, hope fills us beyond the margins and keeps on filling us when we trust in him. We can't be so filled we burst with it, though it can feel like that sometimes. We keep holding out our hands, knowing that God is outrageously and wildly generous, and longs to flood living water over us so we are filled to the brim and more, our faces upturned as we receive the satisfaction we are made for – holy satisfaction. King David, the Samaritan woman and Paul all caught a glimpse of this and, although they were flawed or suffering, they took hold of a secret – but not one they wanted to keep to themselves.

Yearning is holy satisfaction

Satisfaction is wonderful. Rest for our souls is sorely needed. But is that enough, or is there something more, something wilder, something that reaches even deeper into that secret place in all of us? I think there is, and it is to do with the word 'yearning'.

C. S. Lewis's writings often reflect a longing for the things of God. The stories in all The Chronicles of Narnia are of yearning, of characters waiting with bated breath for what they hope will happen. 'Aslan is on the move,' Mr Beaver says in *The Lion, the Witch and the Wardrobe*, and as he breathes the words, something awakens in the children, weaving captivating tendrils of something they never knew they needed, and yet becomes so obvious in that moment:

> At the name of Aslan each one of the children felt something jump inside . . . Susan felt as if some delicious smell or some delightful strain of music had just floated by her. And Lucy got the feeling you have when you wake up in the morning and realize that it is the beginning of the holidays or the beginning of summer.[3]

In the discovery of this enticing longing, these characters shine with a kind of contentment, manifested in a hope that never fails. Living with that longing ingrains a different kind of satisfaction deep in their souls.

Returning to Psalm 63, we find something similar. Before David writes of how God satisfies his soul, he speaks poignantly of an almost aching longing for God:

You, God, are my God,
  earnestly I seek you;
I thirst for you,
  my whole being longs for you,
in a dry and parched land
  where there is no water.
(Psalm 63:1)

He then writes about how he has glimpsed God's power and glory in the past, tasted of the love that is better than life. It seems to me that he is describing a passionate hunger, a yearning that is sick with desperation. He's separated from the sanctuary, far from the temple and in the middle of the desert, and he knows he needs to be back in God's presence.

The desperate ache of longing

The kind of longing he describes sounds a bit like falling in love – the craving, the pining which takes over your body and soul – as all you can think about is that person. You lose your appetite and your sleep, because you are so very taken up with the intensity of it all. All the colours in the world are brighter, more beautiful; even music is somehow more meaningful. Everything changes.

If we fall in love, we may experience some of these feelings, but they rarely last for years. I love my husband more deeply now than ever after twenty-four years, but I don't tend to toss and turn all night in sighing or desperate pining, thankfully, because he is here with me and I know him so well. With God, though, many do live with something of this heartsick yearning, because, like David, they have caught tantalizing glimpses, been utterly enthralled by the presence of God, but know that they will only be with God fully in the kingdom.

They cannot settle yet into an abiding and comfortable kind of love – the love they have for God, while long-lived and steadfast, is tinged with the kind of ache that comes with the flush of first love.

Pursuit of God is a passionate chase, a thirst rooted in our souls, which we know can be alleviated only by the presence of God. Glimpses of God – the touches we receive, the encounters we taste, fleeting though they are – only serve to make us eager for more, and in that desperation, we move closer to contentment.

Hold on, though. How can a sense of yearning be anything to do with contentment? Surely, we've just found that contentment is to do with being satisfied in God, so any longing we experience must mean discontentment?

In my experience, a longing-for-God kind of discontentment is not the same as the gaping discontentment we might experience about things of the world, our possessions and human relationships. Instead, yearning discontentment is holy discontentment, which, ironically, is far closer to holy contentment than we might think.

Contentment for a Christian means living in a constant state of holy yearning. It means longing for God's kingdom to come, and to come soon.

The marks of holy yearning

Let's remind ourselves of the hallmarks of this holy yearning that we've seen so far.

In Psalm 63 David sought the Lord with all his heart. He remembered the deeds of the Lord and praised God out loud and in song. He thought about God while falling asleep and used the times awake at night to cling to God with his whole self.

The Samaritan woman responded to Jesus' invitation with a spirit of longing: she asked for the water. And then she went and told others about it.

Paul made it clear throughout his letters that he was longing for Christ. He chose a life of praise and thanksgiving and pursuit after all God had for him and, because of this, was overflowing with hope.

We cannot expect God to satisfy our souls fully – to captivate us – unless we too take time to immerse ourselves in his presence and give thanks, praise, remember and express our belief and hope in the glorious gospel. Taking time to do these things does not always come naturally or easily, and we don't always (or even often) feel like doing them. Yet David found that using his time in seeking God gave him so much more than he could imagine. I too have discovered this in the darker times. If I stray far from God and forget to come before him, then my heart is full of anger and discontentment, but if I approach God anyway, something in me changes. I find soul-rest in the storm.

If we choose not to praise, we lose our sense of holy yearning, soon become swallowed up in apathy, and bitterness can swiftly follow. If we choose instead to believe that contentment comes only in chasing God, then holy yearning will become our shape of life, in good and bad times, a sustaining state in its echoes and whispers of hope and life in its fullness.

While you yearn for God's presence, be blessed with those glimpses, those windows on heaven, times when God works amazing things. When God heals, in mind or body or spirit, when you see the signs of the kingdom that Jesus promised. Chase these things, because in pursuing these, you are pursuing God. Believe in God's miraculous work, because God longs to work in power in your life. Believe even when you don't see, because God loves your heart of faith. And know that one day all will be made right, and that which your heart pines for will be reality, in all its glorious, unimaginable splendour, bringing healing and wholeness, and eradicating pain. Look to that time with hope and faith, and catch hold of mesmerizing impressions with all your heart, always wanting more, always craving and striving for more. More of God, the only one who can truly satisfy.

Prayer

Father God,
May I find my restless heart
At rest in you,
The only one who can satisfy my deepest soul.
Be the strength of my heart,
Better than life,
My portion for ever.
Father, help me to long for you,
To yearn for you, in my dry and weary land.
May my ache for your presence
Fall on me like fresh spring rain,
Drenching me in the possibilities of the greatest love,
In holy satisfaction.
Amen.

Reflection

- How does the story of the woman at the well (John 4:1–42) speak to you?
- How does Augustine's quote, 'You stir man to take pleasure in praising you, because you have made us for yourself, and our heart is restless until it rests in you', resonate with you? How is your heart restless?

- Reflect on Psalm 63. Ask God to speak to you through the words, and to fill you with the same senses of both satisfaction and longing that David had.

11. CAPTIVATED IN DARKNESS

When I prayed, I was stranded in a desert, nothing on the far horizon but unrelenting sand and oppressive sky. However much I tried, I couldn't break through. I couldn't find God anywhere, in any direction or in any discipline. I worshipped and gave thanks, and there was nothing. I read the Bible and Christian books, and there was nothing. I looked for the captivating intimacy I remembered, and there was nothing.

I've been through a few of these times. I've sought closeness with God, gone through the motions. And there has been a big brick wall. Thick darkness weaving around my head. I can't see through it and I can't feel through it.

I have struggled to be contented in times like these – times when God's promises of peace and living water seem so far away. So unattainable.

The dark night of desolation

Sometimes we faithfully pray and choose to worship God, but don't experience any positive 'feelings' – of satisfaction, yearning or anything else. We read words like joy and delight and intimacy and love and thirst, but none resonates with us, because all we can see is a great black hole of nothingness.

Perhaps, though, we need to restore a balance for ourselves, between our expectations of knowing God in our emotions and trusting God in our minds. It's wonderful to experience a tangible sense of God, but there are times when he moves us on and teaches us about faith without sight – or touch. These can be painful and often bitter times, but many go through them and discover that they need not be so wrapped up in darkness that no light can be seen.

Christian thinkers have testified to such isolating experiences through the ages. Jesuit priest and author, Jean-Pierre de Caussade, wrote about times of desolation, thinking of them as a stage in coming through to maturity in holiness. God no longer walks before us in obvious light, our path shining in his presence, but stays behind us, unseen but urging us on along the path he has for us. Pursuit of God in this dark night can be much more difficult, but because of that, much more profound, with effects in eternity.[1]

What an intriguing and yet consoling picture – God is still with us, but in a different, more concealed, position, encouraging us forward. Still there to catch us if we fall.

Mother Teresa famously spoke about her 'dark night', which lasted almost half a century. She was unable to experience God's presence, seeing nothing but choking darkness. At first, she began to doubt God, but as time went on, she came to a more seasoned faith where she was able to find ways to live with the darkness, and to embrace God more fully than before. I can't imagine how difficult this was.

Most people won't go through such a prolonged period of nothingness, but many of us will have some experience of it at some time or another, and so need to find the tools to cope with it, even to embrace it as a crucial stage in our journey – a stage that will lead to maturity and contentment.

Downcast souls and waterfalls

It can start so suddenly.

You wake up one morning and the light has gone. Departed from you, leaving you plunged into desolate darkness. You scrabble through the murk and try to put the light back on, but it won't work. Nothing.

All around you it seems like others are revelling in the presence of God and living their days in a kind of exquisite heart-knowledge of God's power and love. You think there must be something wrong with you, that you have done something to make God leave you all alone. Or that God isn't there at all, and you've got it all wrong.

It can be an isolating, desperately lonely time, sometimes made worse by the well-meaning comments of others: 'Is there some unconfessed sin in your life?' 'You should claim these verses of Scripture every day, and then you'll be fine.' 'It's because you need to pray for healing more.' 'Try getting up at 6 am every morning to pray.'

But it's not that simple. Darkness stages can come and go for no apparent reason. Sometimes there will be reasons, but it's the unexplained times when we are seeking God and cannot seem to find him that I want to address here.

A writer in the book of Psalms went through such a period of darkness, and the poem he wrote about it perfectly sums up this experience. The seventeenth-century preacher Jeremiah Burroughs says, 'This is a very good psalm for those who feel a fretting, discontented sickness in their hearts to read and sing.'[2]

As the deer pants for streams of water,
    so my soul pants for you, my God.
My soul thirsts for God, for the living God.
    When can I go and meet with God?
My tears have been my food
    day and night,
while people say to me all day long,
    'Where is your God?'
(Psalm 42:1–3)

This contemplative poem is titled 'A *maskil* of the sons of Korah'. The sons of Korah were probably musicians in the temple, and wrote eleven profoundly meaningful songs of longing and praise to God in the Psalms. It seems that this particular poet was removed from the temple for a time, perhaps with David when fleeing from Absalom.

The writer's sadness increases through the poem as he recalls how things used to be, how he 'used to go to the house of God . . . with shouts of joy and praise' (verse 4). It is clear that he is under a great cloud. In a dark night. He can't see where God is in this, and longs to experience God's presence and power once again. There is a great ache in his spirit, but a pining not only for what he knows will be, but also for what he once had, and this is a burden.

'Why, my soul, are you downcast? Why so disturbed within me?' he continues, calling on his own deepest being. And that's when he makes a decision. A decision to push through, to obey God's command. 'Put your hope in God,' he cries, 'for I will yet praise him, my Saviour and my God.'

In making the shift forwards to praise God, his words begin to flow, in his determination to remind himself of what God has done. He perseveres in worship, and recognizes his brokenness, his inmost soul crying out to God in what must be one of the most hauntingly beautiful phrases in the Bible:

> Deep calls to deep
> in the roar of your waterfalls;
> all your waves and breakers
> have swept over me.
> (verse 7)

He calls to God in an act of surrender, an acknowledgment that God is sovereign, and he has nothing left. His spirit calls out to the fathomless depths of God, deep calling to deep. Even if he can't see God, find him, know him at this moment, his spirit responds to God's Spirit, and he sobs brokenly, prostrate before God, his raw despair laid out for all to see, pounded by the great roar of a waterfall. And then again, ending his poem, he reiterates that he will put his hope in God, he will *yet* praise.

This psalm is about a determined act of the will. The writer doesn't deny his pain or his feelings of abandonment, but gathers them up in his resolve to set God before him instead of letting dismay come between him and God.

In going through a dark night, when we make an active choice to thank God, to remember what he has done and to submit to him, there is an underlying contentment which no pain can shatter – a contentment which may be not a felt emotion, but a firm grounding for our hopes, based in God's sovereignty and promises to be with us always. When we don't make that choice, when we hold to bitterness and turn our gaze from God, our spirits churn with unrest, a discontentment that only turning back to him and affirming, 'I will yet praise you, my Saviour and my God' will alleviate.

A cry in the dark

A darkness fell. A darkness so complete, so all-encompassing, a thick, soupy blackness. From the sixth hour until the ninth hour, it engulfed the land. The darkness of silence, the darkness of desolation: 'About three in the afternoon Jesus cried out in a loud voice, *"Eli, Eli, lema sabachthani?"* (which means "My God, my God, why have you forsaken me?")' (Matthew 27:46).

In the last hours on the cross Jesus was plunged into a darkness so acute that it became a physical reality. But in howling these desperate, wounded words, Jesus was doing something quite remarkable, something that burrows deep into our own experiences of living shrouded in darkness:

> *Torn.*
> Arms spread wide in love-drenched agony.
> Hung in forsaken desolation,
> A blackness of nothing
> Crushing his soul.
> *It is finished.*

Jesus, one with the Father and the Spirit from eternity past, was crushed under a sense of stark abandonment. Taking the weight of sin upon his body, in that moment Jesus felt torn apart from God, in a profound mystery grounded in perfect love. Immersed in darkness, Jesus knew the harshest, bleakest pain that could ever be known, and cried out words recalling Psalm 22, in which David had cried out his own agony to God, in words that explicitly prophesied the cross and passion of Christ. Even though Jesus knew the hope of the end of the psalm – 'He has done it!' (verse 31) – and those present would also have recalled the rest of the words, this didn't soften his present anguish.

In those dark hours Jesus was pressed under the murkiest night. Because of his great sacrifice, we know that in our darkness God has not abandoned us. God's face has not turned away from us – because Jesus bore our sins for us, so that we can be reconciled with a holy God. More than that, God is empathizing with us: Jesus knew what it was to search and find nothing but swirling darkness. Three hours of darkness-drenched agony.

Because of that, our darkness is shattered into pieces – even when we are crying our pain. It's up to us to take hold of what Jesus has done and live in the truth of it, to make an active decision, like the psalmist, to recall God's work in our lives. To live intentionally in the promise that we are never, ever let go of by the great love of God.

God won't let us go, but will help us to grow

But how can we talk of being captivated by God when we're facing something like this? How could the word 'contentment' possibly apply when we are swathed in darkness?

We make a huge shift when we learn to depend on God and believe in his promises, even in the face of doubt and darkness. In that shift, God is bringing us closer to being more like Christ in our humility and surrender to his will in our lives. In such times we move away from a more experiential view of our relationship with God to a more certain and faithful one, where our life with God is dependent not on our sense of his presence, but on our knowledge of who he is and what he has done in our lives – and in the lives of so many millions too.

God longs for us to come to a position where our faith is more important than what we can see or feel. It seems to me that it is in the drier times that we grow more in faith, because we put ourselves aside in our choice to believe *despite*. This doesn't mean that we will one day come to a point where we stop doubting, or where we never question, but that we might come to a more profound understanding of God's work in our lives, and draw closer to the kind of contentment Paul was speaking of, one rooted in so much more than fleeting emotions or experiences – and so much richer for it.

Learning to be captivated by God in our minds as well as our feelings isn't always easy, although some people find this a far more natural process than the idea of 'feeling' the presence of God. Personally, I'd much prefer to experience God in evident power every day of my life, and know his presence all around me like a warm cloak, but I don't. Instead, I'm left in the darkness, and it's up to me to stand on the path that I know leads to light. It's up to me to set Christ before me and surrender. I know that I need not fear that God has forsaken me. He will not turn away from me, for I am passionately loved.

Our darkness is light to God

The first time darkness fell on me I was desolate. I'd built my dependence on a God whom I could grasp hold of, one I could *feel*. But I came to learn that he had so much more for me: he longed for me to be filled with solid conviction as well as the joy of the Spirit.

God longed for me to be captivated by truth.

When I first wrote this chapter, I wanted to give a number of solutions, keen to ease the way for those living in this kind of spiritual wilderness. I wanted to write about a number of spiritual disciplines and how they might help us to build our lives on God in these times – and they can and do, and are worth exploring in more depth.[3] But it became apparent that the agony of darkness can be much more overpowering than a problem to be solved by *x* formula.

What I've learned most of all through my darker times is that although captivated contentment can flood through us when we 'feel' bathed in God's glory, it goes deeper still when it is firmly grounded in the timeless truths laid down in Scripture. And the most important thing to remember when it comes to the thick darkness we sometimes live through is that there is a truth we can cling to with all our might as the storm pounds us: *we can never get away from God's presence.*

Wherever we go, God is there. Even when we think the darkness is too thick and God has departed from us, he is there.

In Psalm 139 David grasps hold of these truths and weaves them into a poem of captivated assurance. He asks God to search his heart, desperate to know God is still near, despite the things he has done. It's as if he is stretching God to the limits in his lyrical lines of longing:

> Where can I go from your Spirit?
>   Where can I flee from your presence?
> If I go up to the heavens, you are there;
>   if I make my bed in the depths, you are there.
> If I rise on the wings of the dawn,
>   if I settle on the far side of the sea,
> even there your hand will guide me,
>   your right hand will hold me fast.
> If I say, 'Surely the darkness will hide me
>   and the light become night around me,'
> even the darkness will not be dark to you;
>   the night will shine like the day,
>   for darkness is as light to you.
> (Psalm 139:7–12)

Even the greatest depths of darkness we experience are light to God. He is not removed by the thick clouds around us, only invisible for a time. We can hold on to these words, knowing that we cannot be separated from God while we are choosing to follow him. We cannot be separated by pain or by suffering, by ill health or by depression, by where we are or what we do. In all our darkness God sheds light; in all our sorrow he draws close.

If we reach out and take hold of these words, we might find that our darkness isn't quite as dark as it seemed. We might find shards of brilliant light blinking through the cracks.

We won't always immediately begin to experience God's presence, or even be granted any kind of instant peace and assurance. But it is worth remembering that this is not all about us. We don't choose to stand on God's words because of the nice feelings they give us, or because they make us feel better. If our motive in worship and study is focused on our present happiness, then we are missing something profound, because worship is about bringing glory to our God. Sometimes meditation on Scripture, worship or prayer will not do anything tangible in us, even for long periods, but how much more will God be glorified if we still make the choice to practise these things? It's an immense step to contentment when we don't use God to make ourselves feel better, but rejoice when he does make us feel better.

And even when he doesn't.

It's through learning to take hold of God's Word – and always setting God before us – that we can catch hold of the profound contentment Paul speaks of.

Even in the dark night of nothingness.

Prayer

Dear Jesus,
I come before you today,
Choosing thankfulness and praise,
Choosing to remember your goodness,
To submerse myself in your greatness,
The depths of you beyond comprehension.
Even when I can't sense you,
When there is a brick wall of nothing,
May I know beyond doubt that you love me,
That you are calling me onwards,
In the roar of a mighty waterfall
Closing around me and over me until I know nothing
But a love
That surpasses everything.
Amen.

Reflection

- Have you experienced times when you felt no sense of God's presence? What did they feel like, and how did you get through them?
- Read Psalm 42. Think about the writer's desperation to know God's touch on him again, like before, and reflect on his decision to praise God in this spiritual desert.
- Meditate for a time on Matthew 27:45–46. Ask Jesus to reveal the full impact of his experience on the cross, arising out of his love for you.

12. CAPTIVATED BY SURRENDER

In the spring of 1820 a tiny baby girl lost her sight due to poor medical treatment for an eye infection. That baby grew up with a determination to create poetry and write stories, and eventually wrote more than 8,000 songs and hymns. That blind baby became the famous hymn writer Fanny Crosby.

So many of her songs were loved and featured in hymn books that Fanny had to write under several different pen names, so the volumes didn't seem taken over by her. Many people were amazed that as someone who had never been able to see, she was able to write so much, and even more amazed by her consistent attitude of happiness and courage. A preacher once told her that he thought it was a great pity that God didn't give her sight, but she responded that if she had been able to petition God before she was born, she would still have asked to be blind. 'When I get to heaven,' she said, 'the first face that shall ever gladden my sight will be that of my Saviour.'[1]

Fanny talked much of her contentment in loving and worshipping her Lord, and had discovered what it meant to be satisfied in God – particularly in submitting herself to his sovereign will:

> Perfect submission, perfect delight,
> Visions of rapture now burst on my sight;
> Angels descending bring from above
> Echoes of mercy, whispers of love.
> Perfect submission, all is at rest
> I in my Saviour am happy and blest,
> Watching and waiting, looking above,
> Filled with His goodness, lost in His love.[2]

These powerful words express a sense of being in a place of complete rest in God's love. It is evident that to Fanny Crosby, being satisfied in God was a natural result of deciding to place him first. The refrain summed up her outlook on the life she was called to live: 'This is my story, this is my song; praising my Saviour all the day long.' It's clear that she practised spiritual disciplines and caught hold of the kind of satisfaction we explored earlier – the holy kind.

But her story could have been so different; it could so easily have been one woven with bitterness and despair, shot through with disappointment that God had left her with no sight. But she turned any bitterness around in the act of submission: in laying herself down, how she was raised up.

Surrender is a contented word

To worship God in spirit and truth means to surrender to God. With all that we are.

Do you struggle with that thought?

I certainly have done.

The seventeenth-century preacher Jeremiah Burroughs (whom we met earlier) defined Christian contentment as 'that sweet, inward, quiet, gracious frame of spirit, which freely submits to and delights in God's wise and fatherly disposal in every condition'.[3]

'Surrender' and 'submission' are difficult words, especially in the mindset of our modern me-focused culture. The word 'submit' conjures images of doormats and whipped puppies rolling over, or a dutiful 1950s housewife. A picture of someone far from free. Yet God's Word suggests that freedom is to be found in the very act of yielding to God, something that we noted earlier.

My experience is that when we let go of our own selves – our shrieking, resisting, defiant selves – and subject ourselves to God's sovereign rule, there we can learn contentment, for we cannot find it in rebellion against him. God knows all we need and has made us for love. Surrendering to God means submersing ourselves in an ocean of that perfect love. It means walking far from the shore, sinking deeper as we wade further in, and the deeper we sink, the more of ourselves we can let go. And the interesting thing is that, as we sink into God's love and God's authority, the less we worry about holding on to those things we were so desperate to cling to, and the more we become liberated to be the people God created us to be.

Jesus' mother Mary surrendered herself entirely to God when the angel Gabriel approached her with God's plan. 'I am the Lord's servant,' she said. 'May your word to me be fulfilled' (Luke 1:38). She abandoned her will, despite the catastrophic ramifications she could surely envisage: she was an unmarried virgin. She knew what her society would think about her pregnancy. She knew that Joseph, her betrothed, would probably walk away, yet there was no trace of complaint, only captivated surrender – a joyful embracing of God's will for her, a certainty that God would bring about good. I love Mary, because she modelled holiness in a tough situation by making a choice. God was the one she wished to please, and she chose him over her own comfort. Yet she never looked like a doormat, or a woman bowing to male domination. She looked like a woman who knew her mind and her heart, a woman who had found freedom in following God's will. A strong woman who made a resolute decision that would echo through history and eternity. I can't wait to meet her!

Captivated contentment can be fulfilled only by absolute surrender, in submission that puts aside everything but true and holy worship. And in that submission comes liberation.

Captivated in fetters of iron

Another woman who lived out captivated surrender despite adverse circumstances was Amy Carmichael (1867–1951). She travelled to India and set up an orphanage to house young girls rescued from temple prostitution and other forms of slavery. Her life was all action and passion for God, but in 1931 she suffered a devastating fall which left her with internal damage and crippling pain, and a condition called neuralgia – a disease of the nerves that rendered her incredibly weak, often consigned to her bed for weeks and months on end.

In the introduction to his collection of Amy's essays on closeness to God, David Hazard says that Amy learned a spiritual secret early in life 'that caused her spirit, if anything, to blaze even brighter in spite of the many difficult circumstances'.[4]

Amy came to realize that being a follower of Christ didn't make her like a jewel encased in velvet, protected from scratches and wear – immune to pain. In fact, to Amy, the Christian life was more about living in a battle and learning to fight, clothing herself in spiritual armour.

I'm struck by this impression of a frail, vulnerable sick woman, laid up in her bed, yet a glorious warrior, clothed in the blanket of faith, the nightgown of righteousness and the nightcap of salvation, the pen of the Spirit and the dressing-gown belt of truth, feet shod in the slippers of the gospel of peace. We don't picture that image when we think of a mighty armour-clad soldier, do we? But what a moving image of a person in pain but so very whole, caught up in her Saviour's love and grace, choosing to arm herself against the insidious words of the enemy instead of arming herself with bitterness. And how beautiful were her slipper-clad, aching feet, announcing the happy news of peace and salvation to so many.

A twentieth-century blogger

Even through constant pain, which she referred to as her 'fetters of iron', Amy continued to write devotional books and poems, pouring out words suffused in God's power and truth. These astute words are as hard-hitting and relevant now, penetrating our outer shells, the masks we put on. They drill down to the sheer core of our identity and our human brokenness.

Amy wrote of an 'upward-facing heart'. In everything she tackled, all she looked at was God, and all her actions were for his glory. God was fully enough, wholly satisfying, all she needed. She spoke of 'the evil whisperer' hissing discontentment at her, encouraging her to wish for better, and how she turned to God instead, hid herself in God, asking God to make pure the inmost desire of her heart. Peace flooded over her as she prayed. 'A spiritual secret is to learn contentment with the things God doesn't explain to us,'[5] she said. On describing her ongoing pain, being bedridden for years, she said that in acceptance she found liberty, victory and peace, but that this acceptance didn't mean acquiescence, and neither did it mean that she believed that God sent these evil circumstances. But it did mean surrender.

> It did mean contentment with the unexplained. Neither Job nor Paul ever knew (so far as we know) why prayer for relief was answered as it was – with long, initial silence. But I think they must now stand in awe and joy.[6]

Amy's secret to contentment was in her relinquishing of control and understanding. She found that in accepting what had happened to her – without accusing God or thinking he had deliberately brought such infirmity on her – she was able to experience peace. And further than this, she drew most strength from her worship of God, in 'tucking herself in' to his love – a wonderful picture of both submission and trust, like a small child folding his body into his mother's arms.

Many of us in twenty-first-century Western culture will struggle with this concept of 'just trusting' God, and not having to understand why. But it is God's invitation – and instruction – to us in many places in Scripture. Job's friends were just as outraged and horrified as anyone in our time would be, berating Job for not asking more of God, not charging him with wrongdoing, or giving God a telling off for not revealing the reasons why Job suffered so. But God's answer was to look at God. Look at God's sovereign work in creation, his ingenuity in all that has been made. Look at this, and you might find you don't need to know quite as much as you thought you did.

Laying down our pride and our incessant thirst for knowledge is a tough thing to do, and we so easily rebel against such an idea. *No, God. I need to know.* I need to know why. But Amy's experience was that in the very act of laying herself down, she was raised up, filled with hope and refreshment, while in the midst of suffering that filled her every moment.

Knowledge is good. Reason is good. God expects us to use the faculties we have been created with. But we are also expected to lift God high above these things, and sometimes that is going to mean living in a kind of limbo, a place where we do not, and possibly will not, have answers, but a place where we catch contentment *anyway*.

Surrender is not all about me

Fanny, Mary and Amy didn't surrender to God because they thought it would advance them or give them strength, power or status. Their surrender was born out of a longing to glorify God alone, and so it took on a beautiful holiness. God longs not for 'surrender' motivated by personal gain, but rather for a person who runs headlong after him and lays bare everything in her life before his throne. This can be a wildly difficult thing to do. We don't *want* to say that God can 'have it all'. Sometimes we sing songs that say that we surrender, or give it all, or consecrate ourselves to God, and sometimes we even mean the words, but other times we leave the words suspended in that well-intentioned moment and carry on regardless with our me-focused lives, unaffected and unconvicted by what we have so thoughtlessly sung.

If we want to get serious about living for God, and chasing the peace of God, then we need to be bowing to God, and then maintaining that attitude through every part of our lives, not just in church or in our morning quiet time. I'm speaking to myself as much as to anyone, for it's so easy to compartmentalize God and forget that we said 'I surrender' just the other day.

The only way to get closer to the kind of captivated surrender we've seen in these three incredible women is to work at it. Take the time to pray. Practise the spiritual disciplines. Let's lay down our own need for control, recognition, power and any other things getting in the way.

Surrender is perfect freedom

When Jesus was telling his disciples that he would have to die, he shared a difficult truth. He told them that their lives as his followers would be lives of surrendering their own wills and desires:

> Then he said to them all: 'Whoever wants to be my disciple must deny themselves and take up their cross daily and follow me. For whoever wants to save their life will lose it, but whoever loses their life for me will save it.'
> (Luke 9:23–24)

Moments before, Jesus had been asking them who they thought he was, and Peter had replied that Jesus was the Messiah, the anointed one. Jesus confirmed this, telling them about his path of surrender to God's will – and about the future victory of the resurrection. The disciples would also need to live a life of submission: to deny themselves. Daily make a decision to follow Jesus – into suffering, and even to death. Clinging to their own desires would see them lose their lives.

Walking with Jesus in the way of the cross means we lay ourselves down, but also means perfect freedom. In laying down our motivations, our tendency to seek our own glory, all the things that keep us from living as children of God, we are fully surrendering ourselves. We're flinging wide our arms and saying, 'I'm yours. All of me.' We're giving all we have, not because we think it will bring us something, but because it's all we can do in the face of a God who has blazed through the darkness of the bondage of sin and called us out into marvellous light. We don't surrender out of duty alone, but out of love and gratitude, and that then becomes our delighted duty.

Now Christ lives in us, and those things that bound us so tightly and kept us enslaved are crucified with him. Such a God who desires our freedom can only bring us to a place of captivated surrender, and our response is to fall on our knees with joy.

Even when those knees hurt.

Only when we choose surrender in our daily lives do we begin to plumb the depths and enter into the great mystery of a God who longs to woo and delight us with a love we can't begin to imagine.

Choose captivated contentment. Let God's immense mercy, grace and infinite love flow over you, enclose you, weave through the darkest places in you as you open yourself to the love that never, ever fails.

Choose captivated contentment. Be stunned by God's glory, overtaken by God's beauty, lost in God's love. Be surrendered, and be abandoned, and find that rare jewel.

Choose captivated contentment, and be free.

Prayer

Dear Lord Jesus,
The one who set me free from all that enslaved me,
Draw me closer to you,

Closer to surrender.
May I submit myself to you,
Even when my mind screams at the word.
Abandon myself to you,
Even when I don't understand.
May I know the delight of submission,
The captivated contentment of raising you above me,
The unknown mystery of your ocean of love.
I am yours,
And I give all that I am to you.
Amen.

Reflection

- What do you think about when you hear the words 'surrender' and 'submission'?
- Do the stories of Fanny, Mary and Amy change the way you think at all? How?
- Reflect for a while on Luke 9:18–26. What does it mean for you to say that you will deny yourself for the sake of Christ? Ask Jesus to lead you into freedom from all that has held you back, and soak you with his peace.

PART 4:
CONTAGIOUS CONTENTMENT

Then you will shine among them like stars in the sky
as you hold firmly to the word of life.
Philippians 2:15–16

Contentment.
Self-focused, self-serving . . .
Or outward focused,
God-serving?
Spilling out from our every pore,
Overflowing with truth and light.
Contagion.
Transferable, communicable, infectious, transmittable.
A pandemic of gospel love.
A revival of hope.
What do we offer?
How are we different?
What would they think, in our church?
What would they see, in our lives?
Dazzling light,
Or bitter discontentment?
Whichever we choose,
The caught will become the catching.

13. CONTAGIOUS DISCONTENTMENT

When my daughter was small, she was gifted in the art of The Tantrum. As a two-year-old, it was all about independence, and if I *did* things to her – for example, putting shoes on (of all the terrible parenting!), then we would have a problem. The shoe would be yanked off and thrown across the room with a screeched 'my do it!', followed by a swift removal of the sock as well, just to embellish the point, or just to be Two, really. If I then dared to put the sock back on, simply in my desire to leave the house, things would quickly escalate. The tears would start, the hands would thrash, the legs would kick, the body would stiffen. Ranting and wailing would start against the hands that had *put* things on her feet. She would go into full-on revolt mode against me.

I always knew that she would come out the other side. And out of it she would come, seeking cuddles, shuddering sulky groans still spilling from her mouth. Not against me and all that I stood for with the Sock and the Shoe, but loving me anyway, despite my arbitrary methods of torture. I was still her mummy. In time, I taught her more appropriate responses and helped her learn to do these things for herself, but in those moments, I took her ranting discontentment. Because I loved her.

Her short-lived tantrums were born in all the frustration of toddlerdom. Should we rage and grumble too, or should we accept the shoes and the socks and walk out of the door, our hand in the hand of the one who loves us more than any other?

Tantrums in the desert

It starts so quietly.

A hiss in our ears, a fleeting impression. Something is not right in our deep places. We feel . . . *meh*. Grumpy.

Too much has gone wrong for us. We've worked hard all week, but we've achieved nothing. The milk is off and we heard Jane from Accounts telling John from HR that we're rubbish at our job. And as for church . . . well, don't get us going. That PCC meeting was a shambles. Nobody could agree on anything, *and* the biscuits were only Rich Tea.

So we moan. We gripe and we mumble.

The voice in our ear gets louder. Tells us we have every right to have a dig at Dave, or talk about Kelly behind her back. Shouts to us that we are in the right. It's totally not fair, the way we're treated. And it's right, that voice. We should listen to it. We should make our feelings known.

So we walk through our lives with a grouch for a voice, and we wonder why we are so bitter about everything. We can only hear that one voice, now, bellowing at us, drowning out any still small whispers that might be telling us something different.

Something liberating.

Because a grumbling spirit is a spirit held captive.

The enemy whispers destructive words into our ears when we choose to listen. The more we carp on, muttering through our lives, the easier we will find it is to grumble, until we are grousing about the tiniest of things. And the uglier our spirit grows, the further from shining out with God's love we are. We become contagious – but, sadly, not with contentment.

There's a body of people who act like this in the Bible, spreading their discontentment far and wide: the Israelites, wandering in the desert, never satisfied even when God provides miraculously for them. God listens to their murmurings, soothing them just as I held my daughter in the throes of her tantrum. When the children of Israel have crossed the Red Sea, delivered from their captors, they are all celebration, singing praises for what God has done for them. But their grateful spirit doesn't last long.

They quickly forget God's miraculous provision. Later on, they grumble about food, wishing they had died back in Egypt, because at least there they were given meat (Exodus 16:3). They wax lyrical about some of the foods they miss (cucumber, anyone?). God listens to their grousing and provides manna, but this doesn't bring them contentment. Some try to hide more away for themselves, but are scuppered by their greed turning into maggots.

God is gracious. God always provides. Yet they live as if they have no faith that God will come through for them.

Crafted idols and bashed rocks

It is clear that God is saddened by their discontented spirits. He has given them so much, time and again, only to be rejected and spat at, and ignored in the face of an idol made of gold which they think will do more for them. God even works a visual miracle to stop the Israelites murmuring against Moses, causing Aaron's staff to bud, to blossom and to produce almonds, and instructs that it be placed in front of the ark of the covenant as a sign that will 'end their grumbling against me' (Numbers 17:10).

This doesn't stop the grumbling. They argue with Moses, harking back to the 'good times' in Egypt. They look back with rose-tinted glasses, forgetting the sheer terror of living there, and the fact that God has delivered them. They are discontented in their present, brooding and sulking, confined in their choice to disbelieve that God has plans for their good.

If I'd been God, I'd have left them languishing in the desert, grouching and growling at one another. They can't do anything but criticize him, and their discontented spirits grow uglier by the day. Even Moses succumbs to discontentment, rejecting God's control and refusing to trust in what God says. He rebels against him by striking his staff against the rock in anger, disobeying God's command (Numbers 20:11). The result of this is difficult for Moses: God tells him that because he did not trust, didn't honour God as holy, he won't be leading the Israelites into the Promised Land.

God provides water for the thirsty children of Israel, because he is gracious, merciful and loving. But for moments, Moses disregards God's actions in his own life, and murmurs against him in anger, and for this he pays a severe penalty.

God is serious about rebellion – and makes it clear that grumbling is rebellion.

Audience of one

My children have played varying roles in their school nativity plays, from angels to wise men, from cows to narrators and elephants. (Yes, that's right. Those well-known elephants present at Jesus' birth.) All they wanted on these occasions was for me or my husband to be present, there in the audience, cheering them on, eyes only for them.

A friend gave me this thought-picture when I was struggling with someone talking behind my back, worrying far too much about what it was this individual was saying about me, and what other people might think of me in turn. I was starting to complain about this person. It was all so *unjust*! My friend said to me that I didn't need to worry, for I only needed to play for an audience of one. To be looking out into that audience, eyes roaming the room until I found who I was looking for, the one cheering me on, the one who loved me more than any other. This idea shifted my perspective, for if I lived my life for Jesus' eyes only, complaint would have to flee. It also changed how I thought about this person, whom I could now see in the light of being one of God's image-bearers.

I also found that this notion helped me to leave behind my habit of comparing. Many of us waste a lot of time comparing: comparing our families, spouses, houses, possessions, our phones, our clothes, our bodies, our talents, our money. Comparison truly is the thief of joy. Comparing with others and finding ourselves wanting only devalues what we already have: thinking the grass is greener on the other side, and living as if it is so can indeed make the grass greener on the other side because it fosters discontentment on our side. In many cases, the grass is decidedly not greener in the first place anyway. So many of us browse our social media feeds, sighing over the perfect lives other people seem to achieve so effortlessly. If we allow this to drain our contentment, we are damaging our own relationships. But if we decide that we are playing for an audience of one, we might find that we spend less time comparing and more time 'rejoicing with those who rejoice and mourning with those who mourn' (Romans 12:15).

Go compare? Try no compare. God has put us where we are, right at this moment in time, and what we do in this moment is up to us. Hankering for other people's lives – or even our past lives, as the children of Israel did, cucumbers and all – is an infringement of the commandment not to covet, and we know that God doesn't give these commandments in order to control or bully, but because he knows they will infuse our lives with richness when we follow them.

Humility chases the shadows away

Choosing a life of grumble-avoidance doesn't mean we have to put on a mask and pretend that all is well.

Earlier, we explored the importance of coming before God with our complaints and our disappointment. There's a difference between debriefing about your day to someone you love (or having a tantrum about shoes) and a constant griping state.

Philippians (remember?) is a letter about rejoicing in God, about peace and contentment in God, but it is also a letter about serving others, putting God first, and striving after him in all we do. Paul makes it very clear that the joy, the peace and the contentment come only as a result of the sacrifice, the service and the God-chasing – and the decision against a grumbling spirit.

One of my favourite passages in Scripture is Philippians 2:

Do nothing out of selfish ambition or vain conceit. Rather, in humility value others above yourselves, not looking to your own interests but each of you to the interests of the others.

In your relationships with one another, have the same mindset as Christ Jesus:

who, being in very nature God,
    did not consider equality with God something
        to be used to his own advantage;
rather, he made himself nothing
    by taking the very nature of a servant,
    being made in human likeness.
And being found in appearance as a man,
    he humbled himself
    by becoming obedient to death –
        even death on a cross!
Therefore God exalted him to the highest place
    and gave him the name that is above every name,
that at the name of Jesus every knee should bow,
    in heaven and on earth and under the earth,
and every tongue acknowledge that Jesus Christ
      is Lord,
    to the glory of God the Father.
(Philippians 2:3–11)

I love that the very earliest Christians were sharing this poem together, because it shows that the emphasis of this small band of followers was on humility and the rejection of pride. Humility in valuing others above ourselves, humility in exalting God above all. Paul's radical take on Christian living once again comes crashing through these words: it's not about us; it's about Christ; it's about others. About chasing the interests of others above our own self-interest.

Christ is our greatest example of this kind of contagious humility. He made himself nothing, which is even more extreme than it sounds, because of where he came from. The

Ancient of Days was mocked and scorned and flogged and murdered, and yet did not utter one moaning word. He lamented his sense of separation from the Father, but as we have discovered, lament is far from griping bitterness. Jesus wasn't afraid to display his agony, and so gave us a model of authentic sorrow without resentment.

Because of Christ's unique act of sheer humility, he is now raised high, and every person will one day acknowledge him.

It's against everything we value as autonomous humans to 'make ourselves nothing', but nevertheless, it is what God requires of us. Making ourselves nothing leaves no room for the insidious shadows of grumbling discontentment – only for a contagious soul that will draw others to Christ. And when we empty ourselves and model ourselves on Jesus, we are most fully human, the crown of creation. In throwing off our selfish pride and grumbling spirit, we catch something so much more wonderful.

God takes our whining

Some of us forget God's story in our lives.

We take up a discontented spirit, which feeds on itself, dragging us further and further from God and from others. Perhaps something awful has happened to us, and we rationalize that we have every right to grumble about it.

The good news is that even if we live under the script of discontentment, it doesn't prevent our salvation. The great thing about our God is the overflowing love poured out on us, however we act, because of what Jesus did for us by dying on the cross and being raised to new life. Even when we are lost in discontentment, even when we grumble and groan at God, he loves us. Nothing can stop that love. God is gracious and forgiving, taking our tantrums and patiently teaching us humility.

That doesn't mean we should carry on regardless. Discontentment is wrong and affects all we are and all we do in our lives, and how others see us. We may have tantrums, but it's up to us to grow up and accept God's help and love with joy and gratefulness.

To remember the story.

But how do we live contagiously and authentically as Christ-followers in a discontented world?

Prayer

Father,
When discontentment is a script in my mind,
Will you shatter it into tiny pieces?
Remind me of who I am in you
And humble me.
Make me contagious for you
By the way I value others,
By exalting you, Jesus, to the highest place in my life.
I will remember all you have done
And live for you alone,
The one cheering me on,
Your face shining with joy as I run into your arms.
Amen.

Reflection

- Can you think of a time when you held on to bitterness and discontentment? What happened?
- How does the idea of Jesus as your 'audience of one' speak to you?

- Read Philippians 2:3–11. Reflect on Christ's humility and astounding love for you. Ask God to give you the same attitude in the way you interact with others.
- If your discontentment is keeping you captive, read through Psalm 145 or Psalm 148 a few times and let praise shatter the bitter words in your mind. Ask God to whisper words of life to your spirit.

14. CONTAGIOUS RECONCILIATION

'I don't want to forgive them. Why should I? They hurt me too much.'

My dear friend clasped my hand. 'But you are hurting yourself. You are keeping hold of the pain. Stepping into forgiveness will be stepping into letting go of that.'

I hunched over. 'But they made me feel like . . . like I was nothing, you know? Like I was worthless.'

'I know.'

'Besides, they never said sorry, did they? Why should I pardon them?'

My friend let the silence fall for a few moments, and I squeezed my eyes shut against the tears, the whirlwind of emotion dragging me back into my eleven-year-old self. I saw myself running up the street, a gang of girls from two years above me chasing me, mocking me. Threatening to beat me up. Laughing at my clothes and my hair and everything else about me. Flinging words at me, words which sank too deeply. *Sticks and stones will break my bones*, went the old rhyme, *but words will never hurt me.*

How wrong it was. The words had hurt too much for too long.

I shook my head.

For a long time I struggled to forgive those kids who bullied me in school. As well as living with low self-esteem, I lived with a bitterness which arose from my decision not to forgive. Even when I left that school and moved away, I held my unforgiveness tightly to me, like some kind of shield around me to protect me from further hurt.

The dance of forgiveness

Jill Drake (née Saward) was a champion for rape victims (and sadly died young). She discovered something revolutionary about forgiveness. At just twenty-one years old, Jill had been raped in her own home, a vicarage, with her father and her boyfriend held at knifepoint downstairs then beaten senseless with a cricket bat. On speaking of forgiveness to *The Telegraph* in March 2006, she said, 'It's not a question of whether you can or you can't [forgive]. It's a question of whether you will or you won't.' Expanding on this, she said,

> Of course, sometimes I thought it might be quite nice to be full of hatred and revenge. But I think it creates a barrier and you're the one who gets damaged in the end. So, although it makes you vulnerable, forgiving is actually a release.[1]

Jill lived her life as one freed, as a beloved daughter of God, and, in doing so, brought release to many, many others in her tireless fight to change justice laws around rape. Jill's willingness to forgive after such a traumatic experience speaks volumes about what forgiveness actually means: it's not about letting others off the hook, about saying that you are fine with what they have done – you're not – but it's about letting go, dancing away from the bondage of hatred, the chains that bind you to the person you will not forgive. Jesus modelled this in the most profound way possible when he pleaded with his Father to forgive those who crucified him.

Forgiving someone is not giving that person free rein to walk all over you. It's giving yourself freedom to know contentment.

The box begins to crack

The problem with holding my unforgiveness close to me was that it hurt more. Every time I thought about those tormentors, I was back in the situation, a sickly child with names thrown at her. The names hit me anew and sank in, and I held on to them.

But God longs for our restoration. After I had held those hate-filled words too long, it was God who broke through and led me into the assurance of being wildly loved and valued. A wonderful couple offered to begin a course of prayer ministry where they gently spoke words of Scripture over me, and in this loving ministry my box began to crack and God's words poured into me.

I remember so clearly one afternoon when they prayed that I would be set free from the old words spoken over me, and as they did so, they asked God to replace the old with the new, that I would see myself as God saw me. As they prayed, I experienced a rush of pure love, like a heat pulsing right through my head, then my chest, as the words of God's love in my mind began to impress themselves on my heart.

Letting go and praying blessing

Saying the words was soul-deep powerful.

Saying the words began the process of setting me free from bitterness and the effects that unforgiveness had had on me. The words did not give these kids a pardon or make them into blameless people; they made me different instead. They replaced bitterness with a lightness of spirit that skipped through my soul. And they did something else as well. They changed my perceptions of the people involved. Saying the words gave me something of God's heart of infinite love and grace, and enabled me to pray a blessing on them.

Praying a blessing on those who have hurt us may seem like a daft idea, something you feel you could not possibly do. You may want to wish harm rather than pray a blessing, which is an understandable reaction to pure hurt. But Jill Saward prayed for her attackers. When we pray a blessing, it releases something in us and sometimes something in the person prayed for. I appreciate that this may seem an impossible task in some situations, but I have witnessed events completely transformed and people changed by the decision to do this.

While society might say that we should hold on to unforgiveness, the gospel says that we should freely forgive, and this forgiveness is not dependent on the other party being sorry. Forgiveness reflects God's character, a character brimfull of grace. God's grace is outrageous – it pardons the worst of sinners, and, as Christians, we should reflect that grace in our lives.

Praying forgiveness is praying reconciliation. We don't necessarily have to be reconciled to those we forgive – Jill wasn't reconciled to the men who so brutally attacked her. There are times when physical reconciliation isn't appropriate or possible. We may need to forgive a relative who has passed away, for example, or someone with whom we have no contact. But what we are reconciling is our own spirits with the Spirit of God; in emptying ourselves of bitterness and hatred, we are releasing ourselves into the freedom God lavishes on us. We are reconciled in our inner beings.

But physical reconciliation is crucial in some circumstances, especially within a church community. When Christians are reconciled to one another, when we practise forgiveness with grace, it is the most beautiful thing, because it is following the pattern Jesus laid out for us. We should make every effort to be reconciled with those around us whom we find difficult, those with whom we have had disagreements and even screaming arguments, those we simply don't like.

But it's not always that easy . . .

The Green church and the Red church

Once upon a time there was a pretty church in a pretty village. The people who went to the pretty church were all happy and in unity with one another, and lots of people came to the pretty church because it got a good Mystery Worshipper report. In the pretty church there was a band of very talented (and pretty) musicians and some excellent speakers, and at the top of it all was a top-notch pastor and his very gifted assistant. They agreed on everything, and were so pleased that they followed Paul's teachings in Ephesians about bearing with one another in love. Everything looked great, and the pretty church thrived.

One day in the church council meeting the pastor folded his hands on the table: 'I've decided that we're going to get green chairs for the church. I've prayed hard about it, and feel that green chairs are the direction the Lord is leading us in.

Green chairs are obviously not the safest choice, but God expects his church to take big steps of faith. So the green chairs are going to be our step of faith. We can even begin a marketing campaign about it. I can see it now: Green Chairs – Keen Chairs!' The pastor sat back, satisfied, waiting for the cries of acclaim and support.

But his assistant chimed in, a frown creasing his brow. 'No, no, Pastor. I'm afraid you've got that wrong, 'cos I've been praying too, and God has told me very clearly that we should go ahead with new red chairs. We need to listen to all those who feel they cannot move beyond red, let alone to something as radical as green! We might lose them – we can't just go ahead and change things so . . . so militantly. No. We must go with red. Red Chairs – Fed Chairs!'

The pastor frowned deeply. 'But if we stick with red, we're not even changing anything.'

The assistant smiled. 'It's a slightly different shade. That's plenty enough.'

As the meeting went on, the council began to form two factions: the Greens and the Reds. The Greens thought that the Reds were stubborn old stalwarts, and the Reds thought the Greens were uncaring anarchists. As time went on, the factions drew further and further away from one another, and forgot to listen to one another. They forgot about patience and gentleness and kindness, and about all the other fruits they once held so dearly in their pretty church. They forgot about anything but winning, because their side was Right.

The sad day came when the Greens left the pretty church to go to start their own pretty church in the next village, where they had their green chairs and painted all their walls green too in an act of Prophetic Courage. The remaining Reds were left with their faded red chairs, and they threw anything with any green overtones out of the church. It did mean they had to replace the vacuum cleaner and repaint the toilet, but none of that mattered, because they were Right about this.

Tragically, the Green church and the Red church stopped being pretty and ceased thriving. No-one wanted to come any more, and when a mystery worshipper reported on them, the result was rather scathing, using words like *unwelcome, conflict, disunity*. The Green church members turned against one another about which projector was the best, and the Red church started flinging hymn books at one another in the midst of heated disagreements about whether to use the old or the new words.

Both churches fell apart and both churches died, and all that remains is a pile of red and green chairs that nobody wants. Most people from both churches went to different churches but didn't like those either, because they used different colours still. They never found anything that really suited them.

The end.

Disunity is murmuring discontent

Now, tongue-in-cheek though this tale is, we can probably all recognize elements of our own churches in it, and how we can sometimes treat one another. Many things conspire to increase our discontentment. One of the most insidious is disunity among Christian people. If we are not at peace with one another, we can all too easily miss out on contentment.

Unity is a symbol of the kingdom, a sign that God is at work among us, blessing our work and taking us forward into his purposes. Disunity leads to murmuring discontentment, conflict and sometimes hatred.

Why do we find unity so very difficult, and reconciliation at times impossible?

Discontentment causes fights and arguments. The people in the Green and Red churches had somehow lost themselves to a brooding sense of discontentment in what they had, and a certainty that they were the ones in the right. When we give in to our own thirst for money, for power, for a sense of importance, conflict can snake its way into our churches, shattering relationships and destroying our witness and our mission to those outside the church.

The enemy delights in conflict, particularly in the trivial ways conflict can start: when we allow ourselves to talk without grace to someone, or send a passive-aggressive email, when we think we are right and decide we don't need to listen to others who are wrong, when we make an accusation against someone without due evidence.

When we do anything without love.

Satan revels in our petty squabbles, our annoyances at one another, and twists himself round them, burying them further within us until we're caught in a negative cycle from which we can't extricate ourselves without a lot of effort. That's why so much of Paul's focus is on unity in the body of Christ. He himself became involved in these kinds of arguments, and realized they were damaging. Look above all that, he said. Look to Jesus. When he wrote to the Corinthian church, a hotbed of factions and conflict, particularly addressing those who had split themselves off, one group to follow him, one to follow Apollos, he advised them to stop deceiving themselves: 'If any of you think you are wise by the standards of this age, you should become "fools" so that you may become wise. For the wisdom of the world is foolishness in God's sight' (1 Corinthians 3:18–19).

Paul confronted their arrogance, their certainty that they were right. In a church in a city renowned for its wisdom, this was a bitter pill to swallow for the Corinthians, but an important lesson to learn. In laying their pride aside, they were more able to embrace the appeal 'to be perfectly united in mind and thought' (1 Corinthians 1:10).

Paul reminded them that God's kingdom is topsy-turvy when it comes to the wisdom of the world. God surprises us with radical, messy inversion. The first are last and the last are first; the wise are foolish and the foolish are wise.

Living in unity is part of thriving in that upside-down kingdom of abundant grace.

It is not possible to be contented in Jesus when we are in contention with others. We cannot hold on to perfect peace when we are fighting with our neighbour. We can't be soaked in the presence of God yet scream obscenities at those with whom we disagree.

Even if we're right and they're wrong.

Disagreeing well

This doesn't mean that we should never disagree with others. Disagreement can be positive and healthy if it is done well. While it's good to suppress our own sense of pride for the sake of others, it's not always healthy to pretend that we don't have a dispute with anyone in the name of loving our brother or sister. Paul made it clear that he confronted Peter when they disagreed on things. The key is to find a good way to disagree. To take our difference of opinion with gentleness and humility to the individual concerned and reject the temptation to gossip or slander behind that person's back. One of the worst things we can do is send emails, copied to anyone we think might be involved, full of barbed comments and self-pitying umbrage. Things only go downhill from there.

Disagreeing is not wrong in and of itself, and there are situations where there is not a 'right' or a 'wrong', as in the chairs story. In this kind of scenario the question to ask is how we as Christians demonstrate Christ's love and grace to one another – could we possibly take a step back and agree to disagree, or even let the other person 'win'? The gospel of Christ, of course, runs counter to the idea of winning an argument, so if we hold winning too dearly, then we are forgetting to surrender ourselves to God.

Perhaps another question to ask is about how we see church: do we see it as God's church, or 'our' church? The danger is evident: we don't want to change things in our church because it belongs to us, and maybe because we have done so much for it over the years. But Scripture lights another way, where we not only surrender ourselves, but surrender our church. Our church belongs to Christ, so we have no entitlement to be so grabby about it. If we can give our church – and anything we do for our church – over to God, perhaps conflict levels would be lower. Perhaps our church would look more like the glorious bride of Christ she is made to be.

Unity is cascaded blessing

King David was so moved by the power of unity, he composed a poem about it. It appears that he wrote this at a time when some conflict was finally resolved, and his delight is clear:

> How good and pleasant it is
>   when God's people live together in unity!
> It is like precious oil poured on the head,
>   running down on the beard,
> running down on Aaron's beard,
>   down upon the collar of his robe.
> It is as if the dew of Hermon
>   were falling on Mount Zion.

For there the LORD bestows his blessing,
even life for evermore.
(Psalm 133)

The image of overflowing oil is so powerful because this 'precious oil' was used to consecrate a priest. Aaron, the high priest whose descendants continued the priestly line, was consecrated by Moses pouring oil on his head. David calls this to mind as a picture of God's people all living in unity. It is a symbol of holiness, and a sign of God's extravagant grace; though the oil is expensive, it is poured out to overflowing. He continues this striking image of harmony with his description of the dew of Hermon. On the mountain the dew was extensive, making it a green and verdant place, in contrast to the dry wilderness regions around it. Living in unity is living in a place where things grow and thrive, and more than that, a place where the land is rich and overflowing with goodness.

David is linking our choice to live without bitterness towards one another to the lavish outpouring of God's love and blessing. It's in this place of reconciliation, he says, that we will find life for evermore. In deciding to live at peace, we seize hold of God's exuberant generosity and gain rest for our innermost selves. Soul-rest in an abundance of oil and an outpouring of mountain dew.

Living in unity and forgiveness grants us peace and makes us contagious for a gospel in which we are deeply contented. Contagious because letting go of our own hostility demonstrates the unrestricted love of Christ Jesus and causes us to 'shine as stars' in a world which doesn't reconcile. Contented because acts of unity and forgiveness replace the agony of bitterness in our darkest places with the staggering vehemence of perfect peace.

How, then, do we turn inner scripts of discontent and unforgiveness on their heads, and immerse ourselves in the peace that results from shining out like stars to all around us?

Prayer

Father God,
When I am caged in unforgiveness
And in disunity with my brothers and sisters,
Break through my bonds,
Your endless grace and loving mercy
Flowing through me,
Like copious oil and reckless-lavish mountain dew.
Healing my hurt,
Bringing me into the glorious freedom of being your child.
Lead me to a place where I can say *I forgive*,
Even when I don't feel able to.
Liberate me as I dance into the inexpressible joy
Of contagious contentment.
Amen.

Reflection

- Think about the story of the Green and Red churches. How are you willing to put your own wishes and preferences aside to live in unity, so that this doesn't happen to you?
- Are you struggling to forgive somebody? Take some time to read more of Jill Saward's story online, and ask yourself how her words resonate with you. Then reflect on Psalm 133. Ask God to speak to your heart about forgiveness and unity, and to set you free from the bondage you are in.

- If you need to forgive someone with whom you cannot be reconciled, then take time to be in God's presence with the painful memories you have. It may be that seeking counselling would be a good idea for you if the hurt runs so deeply that you cannot even imagine being able to say the words.

15. CONTAGIOUS SHINING STARS

'I wouldn't want to be a Christian,' my friend said. 'When I went to church, they did nothing but moan and complain. No-one seemed happy to be there. All they did was whinge about one another. And then said they were better than everyone else!'

My stomach sank. 'They're not all like that.' But my stuttered words were too weak.

'Well, they are in my experience. Present company excepted, of course. But every church I've been in is the same. They're a load of whiners. They only had time for me when I did something for them as well.'

I nodded along, squirming on the inside.

'Someone even moaned at me for sitting in his seat. Said that's where he always sits, that he's sat there for the past sixty years. I had to get up, gather the kids and all their stuff, and move. And then I could hear moaning about the noise we were making, and about the baby crying. They're nothing but hypocrites. Sorry.'

I forced my mouth into a smile. 'It's OK. I get it.'

But it's not OK. It's not OK that my lovely friend's experience of church is of a place of bitterness and discontentment. It's not OK that the only contagious thing in her experience is grumbling.

It's just very sad.

A magnetic spirit?

Think about a Christian person you rate really highly. Perhaps she has an amazing story to tell, or has gone through something difficult and held to belief in Jesus. Perhaps she has many, many years of faith under her belt. What is the one thing that draws you to her – the thing that commands respect?

In every case I can think of there is something like a softness of spirit, an uncomplaining soul that draws other people to them, a magnetic spirit which is nothing to do with natural personality, but everything to do with a state of heart: a rejection of discontentment. Grumbling and arguing are foreign to the way these people present themselves to the world. Instead, they shine like stars in the sky.

A woman I knew when growing up, Sheila,[1] was like this. She went through too much in her life, losing her dear husband at a young age, unable to have children, suffering painful illnesses, sorrow and rejection, but there was something dynamic about her. Her skin almost shone, a translucent quality that radiated joy. She smiled a lot, and the thing that particularly struck me about her was that she was always concerned for others. Nothing was ever about her, despite her own brokenness. She was full of the Holy Spirit, brimming with grace, yet never tried to cover over what she had been through, or minimize it. What Sheila lived out was a rejection of bitterness and an embracing of her hope in Christ Jesus.

And now she is pain-free in glory, her face shining even more than it ever did on earth.

The Christian mystic Teresa of Avila said,

> The surest way to determine whether one possesses the love of God is to see whether he or she loves his or her neighbour. These two loves are never separated. Rest assured, the more you progress in love of neighbour the more your love of God will increase.[2]

I saw this truth in Sheila's eyes. She'd caught contentment in putting others above herself.

Shining lights or dimmer switches?

But I *deserve* more. I *deserve* better. Why shouldn't I look after number one?

In the last two chapters we've seen how the choice to live in discontentment, disunity and dissension can draw us far from peace. All this is fed by an insidious force, increasing its power the more we sink into its grasp. That force is pride. Pride whispers to us that we don't have enough, that we should have more. Pride scoffs at the idea of forgiving others, and sneers at any kind of submission to others or to God. Pride grows like a weed when the conditions are right, and if we let it permeate our minds and our souls, our spirits are dampened and our hearts churn in restless unease.

All around us the world is whinging, and telling us we should be whinging along with them. We deserve a good old rant. Life is hard! People can be difficult, so we should moan. Get it out of our system, especially if we're having a particularly tough time.

Perhaps it feels too hard not to grumble and complain. We feel like we can't possibly be contagious for the gospel in our situations. We're too weak to shine like stars, so we might as well dim our lights and go for the bellyaching session big time.

But, actually, that's when we can make an active choice to be catching *for* contentment.

I've found that in allowing myself to be vulnerable to others in my own pain – perhaps in requesting practical help, or simply asking people to visit – they become more open to talking about God. I've discovered that I can be contagious in my weakness; I don't need to achieve great things or bound around full of energy to tell others about Jesus. God works in and through where I am, sick and sometimes housebound, and my choice to be both contented and real to others means that they sometimes want to know more.

I've also discovered that I can be just as contagious when I choose bitterness. When I become locked in a cycle of discontentment.

Discontentment is not just to do with complaint. It's a state of mind and heart that can keep us locked in an unhealthy cycle which draws us further and further into negativity. We become hemmed in by it, stewing in our discomfort and letting it build in us and bind us up until we are fermenting rage, unable to see beyond it. Discontentment is self-perpetuating and self-fulfilling, a destructive force which drives us into a desert of bitterness.

Discontentment turns the dimmer switch all the way down.

Grumbling culture vs glorious gospel

The Christians at Philippi were on a long journey to spiritual maturity. While they were fully on board with gospel truth, some had a tendency to moan about everything, as was the norm in their culture, hardly advertising a transformative and powerful movement of God. So Paul advised them to stop:

> Do everything without grumbling or arguing, so that you may become blameless and pure, 'children of God without fault in a warped and crooked generation.' Then you will shine among them like stars in the sky as you hold firmly to the word of life.
> (Philippians 2:14–16)

This instruction comes on the back of Paul's urging to continue to work out their salvation, to go forward in their journey towards holiness. Paul was concerned with how people walked in their faith in daily life, and in turn how this appeared to others, because it was his most fervent desire to bring others into the glorious hope of salvation. Philippi was a society where a contented and non-grumbling spirit would stand out a mile against the restless and disaffected backdrop of the time and place.

It's not so different in our time and in our culture though, is it? Perhaps we're even worse, and tend even more towards complaining, entitlement and general moaning about anything and everything – and, sadly, this can be reflected in our churches, as in the case of my friend's unfortunate visit. Paul's message is just as relevant to us today, and just as world-changing. If we 'shine as stars' in the world, we're going to become contagious for good. Our rejection of discontentment and grumbling will be catching, and our stars will shine brighter.

Paul doesn't just tell us to stop grumbling, full stop. We need to stop grumbling in order to achieve something – to become children of God without fault who will shine out in a dark world full of corruption. The way we can stop our moaning is by holding firmly to the Word of life. Holding firmly on to something is a dynamic choice, something we embrace with all our might. It's running to catch that ball and then holding it tightly. Holding tightly to something means that we hold it dear, that we value and trust it, that we want to keep it. Clutching God's glorious gospel close to us means that we meditate upon it, we feed on it, we tuck it away inside ourselves until we are radiant with the truth of it.

And then we give it away.

Shiny words and actions

But it's just too difficult to be contagious for our faith.

Isn't it?

It is challenging to find words to tell others about it. Many circumstances we find ourselves in don't seem to be ideal for sharing our faith, either for professional reasons or because relationships are fragile and might be ruined if we are forceful. We've all heard stories of Christians who push their faith at others, with no thought for what's going on in that person's life, and subsequently put them off Christianity. It's important to be careful about how we share, and whom we share with.

However, this can too easily become a cop-out. I have some wonderful friends who don't have faith, and I have to admit that I shy away from talking of faith matters, because when I have done in the past, it's been obvious that they're not interested. So I keep it to myself, sometimes hugging it to me like a toddler with her comforting teddy bear, unwilling to give anyone else a chance of a cuddle. They don't want it, after all, I say to myself. I'd only ruin what we have.

There are times when it wouldn't be appropriate to say something. But there are also times when we miss the opportunity through fear and, perhaps, apathy. For if we have caught contentment in Christ, how can we *not* share it? How can we keep it to ourselves? After all, if we'd fallen in love, and that person was amazing in every way, we'd be telling our mates, wouldn't we?

Sometimes it isn't about telling people, but showing them. We demonstrate our faith in how we speak and how we act. It was the actions of the folk in church that hurt my friend as much as the words. God's heart for people is made plain in so many scriptures about caring for those who are vulnerable, seeking justice and righteousness, and loving one another. If we claim to be contented in Christ and yet oppress the needy (or ignore them), then our contentment is not grounded in the depths of who Christ is and what he has done. Jesus turned the world's thinking upside down. He stretched out his arms and launched kingdom values into a community of people, and they were never the same again.

Living as children of God, our actions will hopefully be infused with the love we have received, but there are times when we must go further, with words. The story of Christ's life, death and resurrection was first declared in the four Gospel accounts, and continues to be declared to this day as the only way to God. We need to be uncompromising in the way we share this fundamental truth, relentless in our quest to bring others into the kingdom, and so to a holy contentment.

It's time to decide whether we long to be so passionate for Jesus that our contentment spills over as a result. If we do, we cannot help but serve and witness to others, and so shine as brightly as stars.

Some fruits are shiny

Is it possible to live like that all the time? Should we always walk around with shining faces and sparkling hearts?

The simple answer is probably not. But, as with all things to do with growing in our faith, we can come closer to God's ideal for us by following his commands. Remember how we discovered that the church in Galatia had been hanging on to a rule-based version of Christianity, and so Paul emphasized freedom to them? Part of this freedom came through growing in qualities that helped them draw closer to God – and closer to others: 'But the fruit of the Spirit is love, joy, peace, forbearance, kindness, goodness, faithfulness, gentleness and self-control. Against such things there is no law' (Galatians 5:22–23).

Paul used this list to contrast the result of living by the Spirit with living by 'the acts of the flesh', which lead us away from God and towards bitterness and discontentment (verses 19–21). Paul's emphasis is not that we gain salvation by being kind or doing good works, but that part of coming to know Christ and growing in him means that these fruits will become more and more evident in our lives. The more time we spend with Christ, the more we surrender to and pursue God, and the more we will burst with these contagious characteristics. We're no longer bound under law, because exercising these attributes will both draw us closer to holiness and lead us into freedom. That's why those Christians we called to mind at the beginning of this chapter are so catching: the fruit of the Spirit has become part of who they are. They have sunk their roots deeply into the riches of God's love and grace.

Here's a thought. What if all of us Christians acted out of these fruit at all times? What would the world look like? What would our relationships look like?

It's striking that the first on Paul's list is love. It's always about love, isn't it? Everything comes back to it and sparks from it. All those other fruits take their strength from it, because it is the source of being. God's love invades our sin and our sorrow and weaves contentment around us when we least expect it. God's love shatters our pride and our envy, our grumbling and our hatred, and cascades over us, transforming us once again.

The more we love God, the more our love for others begins to reflect the kind of love God has lavished on us. The more time we spend in God's presence, the more we access his love, freely available when we ask, pouring down over us as he delights in our worship. The more we read God's words of love in Scripture, the more we are assured of how he sees us and feels about us. And the more we access God's love, the more we learn to respond with our own love – which, in turn, shapes our love for those around us.

God's love is perfect and infinite, so loving God above all extends perfect and infinite love into the lives of others.

Love comes into every choice we make every day. Every time the phone rings or the boiler fails or the toddler stamps his feet, whether we are on hold to our utilities company or HMRC,[3] who don't seem able to grasp what we are saying, or stuck behind someone pootling along an A road at thirty-five miles per hour, or sitting in a church business meeting talking about the possible colour of the new chairs. Are we going to do all these things without grumbling, or will we give in to that voice inside us – the irritation springing up, threatening to spill over?

If we really do hold the love of God and God's Word close to us, hidden in our hearts, it will shine from us, pouring forth from us in everything we say and do. In turn, the more we demonstrate this love to those around us, the more we will love God – and contentment will flow from that intensity of love.

Love ablaze, shining from us and soothing the depths of us. Love extravagant, distilling our fear and pitching turmoil far from us.

We just need to chase that love . . .

Prayer

Dear Lord Jesus,
When I am bitter and long to grumble,
May I know your abiding presence
Holding me close,
Gently encouraging me to shine,
To hold to the Word of life
Which brings freedom.
Help me to radiate your light to all around me
Through all my words and all my actions.
Pour out your infinite love over me,
Through me,
Until I can do nothing but love.
May I reflect you in the fruits of my life,
Be contagious in my contentment.
Amen.

Reflection

- Is your spirit magnetic?
- Think about your church. Is it a place where grumbling has taken hold, or a place where the light shines brightly to all who come through the doors? How can you help spread that light even more widely?
- Reflect on Philippians 2:14–16. Ask God to reveal the state of your spirit, and to fire you with a desire to be contagious for the Word of life.
- Read Galatians 5:22–23. Take some time to think about what each of these 'fruits' looks like. If you're a creative type, represent them in artwork or poetry, or simply take time to meditate on them.

16. CONTAGIOUS GOD-CHASING

A while ago I was trying out a new series on Netflix. I'd heard some good reviews and was keen to watch it – the story sounded like it would be up my street. However, halfway through the first episode I began to feel drained, like the air had been sucked out of the room. It felt like my spirit was being battered, trying to hide away from images on the screen that weren't in any way lovely, admirable or good. I knew the Holy Spirit was working in me to make me aware that this programme was not good for me. Even the episode I saw sent me into a darker place than I was in before.

So I took the series off my watch list.

Chasing the thing

We want the thing.

The thing that will satisfy us. That will plug that empty space, fulfil us, connect us.

We search for it. We hunt high and low. We keep pursuing it, and when we look in the wrong places, we create more empty spaces, so we seek more stuff to lift us out. To take us above. To forget.

When we forget to chase the good, we bring unrest crashing down on our souls.

Things in this world can be brilliant. Music, art, literature, comedies that make us laugh out loud, stunning cinematography, the good that others do, the beauty of nature, making our environment attractive, helping those less fortunate than ourselves. There is much that upbuilds and inspires, brings hope and joy.

There's also the stuff we can all too easily slip up on. So much in our society is ugly and binding, dragging us into despair rather than hope.

Porn use is at an all-time high. There is an unprecedented level of addiction to porn, which starts very young, with access to ever-darker stuff on the web. It's now proven that addiction to pornography actually changes the brain, altering dopamine levels, which has a negative knock-on effect on actual relationships. I've heard people – even people of faith – minimizing the effect of porn, maintaining that it's only harmless fun. It's not.

The truth is that what we fill our minds with can do harm or good, and if we are filling our minds with images we know are not pleasing to God, then they will damage us in our inner beings.

The problem is, it's so very easy to become immersed in things that do us no good, to get swept up by the waves which engulf us and leave us with nothing but a heart of restlessness. We begin to believe what society tells us, that there is no harm in it, that we shouldn't deny ourselves a bit of fun, that these things enrich our lives because they make us feel happy. And as soon as we start to think this way, we remove ourselves further and further from the living light which is the gospel of Christ. We become steeped in darkness and wonder why we feel dissatisfied, but we are so reluctant to turn back to the light, because it might mean giving up something we like doing. It might mean surrendering our will.

The secret of contentment

Paul has found the thing.

In Colossians 3 he sets out his mandate for holy living. We put our earthly natures to death, for we have been raised with Christ. We must reject evil, for we have taken off the old self and put on the new. 'Set your minds on things above, where Christ is,' he says (Colossians 3:1). In doing this, we will become clothed with 'compassion, kindness, humility, gentleness and patience' (verse 12), and then over all those things, put on love (verse 14).

The new followers of Christ in Colossae were in danger of being led astray by 'hollow and deceptive philosophy' (2:8). They were taught that the wisdom of this world was what they needed, rather than looking to Christ. Paul rushed in and subverted this kind of thinking. It was in setting their minds on things above that they would find freedom, not on earthly things.

When Paul wrote this letter, he was in the same situation as when he wrote to the struggling church at Philippi – imprisoned and under a possible death sentence. Yet both letters express his utter freedom in knowing Jesus.

The whole of the fourth chapter of Philippians leads up to Paul's statement that he has found the secret of contentment. He reminds us about the importance of unity, and then about rejoicing in God, remembering all God has done, praying with thanksgiving instead of living with anxiety.

And all this leads to the intriguingly assuring declaration that 'the peace of God, which transcends all understanding, will guard your hearts and your minds in Christ Jesus' (Philippians 4:7).

The next two verses give us one of the most crucial keys to unlock contentment:

> Finally, brothers and sisters, whatever is true, whatever is noble, whatever is right, whatever is pure, whatever is lovely, whatever is admirable – if anything is excellent or praiseworthy – think about such things. Whatever you have learned or received or heard from me, or seen in me – put it into practice. And the God of peace will be with you.
> (Philippians 4:8–9)

Yet again, this is about a choice. The process of being made holy involves learning to focus our minds on good things. Paul is not insisting that we never look at 'worldly' things – he's not saying we should gaze at images of heaven or listen to worship music all day, every day – but he's encouraging us to seek the good things. The praiseworthy things, the admirable things, things that make our spirit sing.

God created the universe and created human beings to bear the divine image. It makes sense, therefore, that things that are good, excellent and lovely reflect his character, his creativity and his goodness. And things that are not good reflect the enemy.

Where do you want to spend your time – and what do you want to put into your mind, body and spirit? This is not a gentle suggestion, a nudge in the right direction with a wink in acknowledgment that it is just too difficult. This is a command, a directive for a life lived in contentment. It is only in chasing after the good that the restless places in us will be stilled.

God is no killjoy

God doesn't ask that we focus on good things just to give us rules we must obey, to take away our pleasures in life or to make us over-pious. God knows what our souls hunger for. He knows the best things for our spirits, and so how we can find contentment.

For me, that particular programme on Netflix was a no-go area; for others it possibly wouldn't be. It's up to each one of us to exercise both common sense and our knowledge of the Word and the Holy Spirit in order to make everyday choices. We get to know the voice of the Spirit speaking to us if we are open to God, and we know instinctively when we have started to focus on something unhealthy. The more we practise holy contentment, the more we come into line with God's hand on our lives, able to discern that still small voice guiding us into all truth.

I love that God knows what we need, what makes us thrive and flourish, and what fills us with joy. I love that he is not a killjoy, not the stereotypical cartoon character God who sits on a cloud and sends thunderbolts against those who are naughty. I love that he is a God of fun and joy and friendship and beauty and grace and purity and excellence, and that he wants us to pursue these things for our good, not to reprimand us or make us joyless doormats.

God is all about bursting extravagance and reckless, joy-breathed love. And that's what he longs for us to know in the very deepest places in us. That's why God holds it out for us. Hurls it in our direction with passion and delight.

We only have to hold out our hands.

Godliness with contentment

Paul knew the secret.

One of the best-known passages on contentment in the Bible comes from his first letter to Timothy: 'But godliness with contentment is great gain' (1 Timothy 6:6). Paul was warning Timothy about teachers who were sharing false doctrines, filled with pride about themselves and spreading strife, envy, malicious talk, evil suspicions and constant friction (verses 4–5). These teachers saw 'godliness' as a means to financial gain, but only the appearance of godliness – or what they saw to be the appearance of godliness, which was really nothing like godliness at all. The mark of these people was conceit; they decided that they knew better, that they didn't need to listen to 'sound instruction', but instead got caught up in petty controversies, and arguing their point became more important than anything else. They were contagious for negativity and arrogance instead of for godliness. They did not look to the good. They did not chase God.

Paul made the statement about godliness with contentment to shut down these charlatans completely. Godliness, he wrote, was nothing to do with appearances, but a state of the heart.

Contagious godliness looks like a heart after God. It looks like chasing the good and the right. It looks nothing like keeping up appearances or the love of money.

It looks like contentment.

There is nothing more catching for faith than a life lived for Christ without borders, a life lived in all-consuming passion, blazing with vitality and overflowing with unconditional love. Such a life lived in godliness and contentment is so powerfully contagious for the kingdom that its effects reach far into eternity.

Chase the good. Be passionate about what God has put in your heart. Yearn for the beautiful, the pure, the admirable. Be radical in your private life: throw out those things binding you so tightly inside, and embrace the joy God longs to pour down over you, pounded by a waterfall of grace.

#Blessed

A word to capture happy moments, to proclaim something good in our lives. It's become a bit of a bland word in our culture, though, so often liberally scattered over filtered images of perfect homes on Instagram.

But Jesus used the word for something more intense. He used the word 'blessed' to describe a state of being for those who are following God with all their heart, soul, mind and strength. Blessed-minus-hashtag means an overwhelming sense of rightness and peace, which goes far, far deeper than a quick smile or clicking a 'like' button.

Jesus talked about the heart-deep blessing we receive when we live in a way that prioritizes the kingdom and subverts the values of the world. In one of his best-known speeches, he spoke to his disciples about blessing that doesn't arise from circumstances, but from chasing after the good, and living for God's values:

> Blessed are the poor in spirit,
>   for theirs is the kingdom of heaven.
> Blessed are those who mourn,
>   for they will be comforted.
> Blessed are the meek,
>   for they will inherit the earth.
> Blessed are those who hunger and thirst for righteousness,
>   for they will be filled.

Blessed are the merciful,
for they will be shown mercy.
Blessed are the pure in heart,
for they will see God.
Blessed are the peacemakers,
for they will be called children of God.
Blessed are those who are persecuted because
of righteousness,
for theirs is the kingdom of heaven.
(Matthew 5:3–10)

I love how this is echoed in some of the things we have explored from Paul's writings: the ideas of humility, of pursuing justice and righteousness, the importance of forgiveness. Right here, in these words near to the start of Jesus' earthly ministry, he was emphasizing the connection between suffering and contentment. He was telling the disciples that even though they *would* mourn, and they *would* be persecuted for their faith, they would receive a blessing that would somehow outweigh the pain. Jesus never denied the pain, but in a glorious about-turn of the thinking of the world, he afforded the pain a depth of contentment they could never find in anything else.

Jesus was all about contentment in scandalous, extravagant kingdom principles. Principles of throwing our arms open and walking into a God-chasing life of servanthood rather than selfishness.

Jesus: the most contagious of all

Jesus lived in the most profound and enveloping contentment any human being would ever know on earth. He was in complete unity with his Father's will, delighting in his Father's presence. He embodied peace, embracing each minute as a holy moment. He lived out fulfilment in his love-drenched interactions with others, in relationship and in serving. All his actions were seasoned with grace. Jesus practised wild generosity and longing, utter serenity and deep compassion. He was passionate, life-enhancing, radical, countercultural and always played for an audience of one. He lived a life of integrity, courage, honesty, hope, suffering and perfection.

Jesus would become a man of sorrows, heavy with suffering, a human being who would undergo the very worst of pain and shame. Yet he chose submission in doing God's will during the greatest test, the most hideous personal cost.

Jesus gave us words of rich, life-giving power, which would lead to something of the contentment he experienced. 'Peace I leave with you; my peace I give you. I do not give to you as the world gives. Do not let your hearts be troubled and do not be afraid,' he said in John 14:27, addressing the sense of longing and the discontentment deep in our hearts. He whispers those words to your heart now, speaking peace into your soul. He holds his nail-scarred hands out to you, breathing rest over your troubled places.

Jesus first said these invigorating words to his disciples, longing to comfort them because he knew what was coming. He promised that he wouldn't leave them, but would send the Holy Spirit to guide and reassure them and fill them with power. It was the Spirit who would fill them with this indescribable peace, calm their fears and remind them of the words Jesus had spoken over them, the people he would lay down his life for. The Holy Spirit continues to speak these words over you today as he drenches you in the fullest life you could ever know, the greatest adventure you could ever experience.

For 2,000 years now, people have discovered this Jesus afresh. He wasn't just a good man who travelled around saying nice things in first-century Palestine; he is the Son of God. The words he spoke apply as much to us today, and his actions, so saturated in pure love, are as much for us to imitate in our lives. Jesus has stood the test of time, his grace-filled love streaming through history, gripping hold of millions upon millions who turn to him. Jesus' death and resurrection story still seizes our hearts, the truth of his great sacrifice and glorious victory over death penetrating through doubt and fear, bringing us to our knees in abandoned worship. There is nothing else we can do in the face of a love of which we can only snatch the smallest, enthralling glimpses, which still floors us with its sheer power.

Take Jesus' words of peace upon you, over you, behind you and before you. Let them seep into your soul and chase old words away, words that would keep you captive but have no place in your life with Jesus at the centre. Snatch these words, hold them tightly and catch holy contentment:

> Peace I leave with you;
> my peace I give you.
> I do not give to you as the world gives.
> Do not let your hearts be troubled
> and do not be afraid.

Prayer

Lord Jesus,
Lord of life,
When my heart turns to those things that leave me
Seething with unrest,
Turn my face back to you.

May I chase the good,
The perfect,
The excellent and praiseworthy,
The beautiful.
You.
Transform my heart,
May it beat for you,
The one who gave everything.
Comfort me by the power of your Spirit
So I may walk in the light of your presence,
Contagious for your glory,
Satisfied in your holiness.
Amen.

Reflection

- Have you experienced the unrest of spirit that comes from pursuing something that is not God-inspired? How did you deal with it?
- Read Philippians 4:4–13. What stands out to you in these verses? Think about the adjectives in verse 8. Which one speaks most to your spirit as something for you to pursue? How will you do this?
- Take some time to reflect on all of John 14. Ask Jesus to speak these words into your heart, and the Holy Spirit to assure and comfort you, and fill you with a perfect peace beyond anything you can find in this world.
- As we come to the end of our exploration of contentment, what are your thoughts? What has changed? You might want to write down some of your impressions, and anything you feel you need to take action on.

CONCLUSION: HOLY SATISFIED

But seek first his kingdom and his righteousness,
and all these things will be given to you as well.
Matthew 6:33

You're breathless, giddy. Eyes fixed ahead of you on the red dot speeding through the sky, growing and expanding as it hurls itself through space. You stretch out your hands, arms flung widely, face turned upwards.

You're going to catch it.

The ball is almost on you. But your hands are in the wrong place. You're too far away. You lurch over to your right, hands held higher, zone in on the target, every last ounce of energy concentrated on the goal.

The ball slams into your waiting hands. Bounces back out of your grasp. You reel, pitch over, grasp the ball a split second before it hits the ground, clap your hands together over it, hold it tightly to your belly.

Phew! You've done it. You've caught it.

You've caught it because you chased it. Because you reached for it. Because you were focused and determined. Because you wanted it so much.

You examine it carefully and find that it's even better than you had ever imagined. It's all you wanted and more.

It's time to throw it to your neighbours. To tell them about the secret.

The depths and heights of a mystery

I wrote this book because a friend asked me to lead a seminar about contentment at a New Wine festival. When she first asked me, I almost laughed. Why me? Why contentment? Why would they want someone like me to talk about something like that? Surely, they would want someone who had an amazing story, someone who was all fixed and buzzing with energy?

But there was that nudge. That small whisper. This was what I needed to do. So I began my journey and discovered a mystery that changed me. It didn't fix me; it didn't make me better, but it did something more than that.

It turned my eyes away from me.

In the middle of his teaching about living as Christians, Paul said that he had learned a mystery. He'd learned the secret of being content in any and every situation (Philippians 4:12–13).

In everything Paul did, Jesus Christ came first. His eyes were firmly and fervently fixed on Christ, and all his strength, all his joy and all his peace were as a result of his single-minded pursuit of Christ. For Paul, it was never about using Christ to feel good, but always about abandoning himself to him – even when that meant hardship. Paul's passion for Christ and for following the ways of Christ led him down a path to contentment, a path of intentional striving and action. Paul caught contentment because he set Christ before him and set all else aside. For him, contentment wasn't about personal feelings, but about the assurance he found in trusting in Christ, and his certainty that Christ is now with the Father, interceding for us.

He caught contentment because he was confident in his faith, courageous in his suffering and brokenness, captivated by the glorious, dazzling presence of his Lord, and contagious in his mission. And Christ was always at the centre of it all.

We, too, can catch the secret when we put our faith in Christ's words and pursue him with our whole selves. When we stop tethering contentment to the escape from suffering and disease and sorrow, or to the idea that God always fixes things when we ask. In choosing to surrender to Christ in these situations, we spread out our hands and experience a contentment that is way beyond complacency, more profound than satisfaction and more lasting than happiness. In chasing Jesus with confidence, courage, captivation and contagion, we enter into the mystery of a God who suffers with us, gathers up our tears, gives us strength and fills us with joy unspeakable.

Because contentment is based not on our wholeness, but on God's holiness.

Filled to the measure of the fullness of God

I can't imagine any better way to close this book than with Paul's prayer for the Ephesians (Ephesians 3:16–21). These few verses sum up the heart of this book and something of the sheer immensity, the absolute magnitude, that is God, and the riches Paul had discovered. They express God's longing for us to be so filled up with joy in the Holy Spirit that we burst with the glimpses of knowledge of God's greatness:

I pray that out of his glorious riches he may strengthen you with power through his Spirit in your inner being, so that Christ may dwell in your hearts through faith.

Amen.

Out of God's glorious riches, too exquisite to behold,
may God restore you with power through the Spirit
in your inmost being.
May Christ Jesus abide in your deepest heart through
faith alone.
May you know this strength which surpasses anything
you can imagine.
May you be filled with a confident faith through
the Spirit of Christ.
May you catch holy contentment.

*And I pray that you, being rooted and established in love, may have
power, together with all the Lord's holy people, to grasp how wide
and long and high and deep is the love of Christ, and to know this
love that surpasses knowledge – that you may be filled to the measure
of all the fullness of God.*

Amen.

And may you who are rooted and grounded in God,
established in the love which never gives up on you,
may you grasp the power God freely bestows,
together with all the saints,
now and for ever through history and eternity –
the power to seize hold of how wide and long
and high and deep,
how immense and immeasurable and boundless
and profound,
how sweeping and towering and soaring and unfathomable
is the love of Lord Jesus.
And may you know this great love that transcends wisdom,
that outweighs knowledge,
that eclipses learning –

that you may be filled to bursting point,
saturated with love unquenchable,
completed with the fullness of God, your God.
May you be utterly overwhelmed with this love
which is so indescribable.
So liberating.

*Now to him who is able to do immeasurably more than all we ask
or imagine, according to his power that is at work within us, to him
be glory in the church and in Christ Jesus throughout all generations,
for ever and ever!*

Amen.

Now to God – to your glorious God,
to God who is able to do immeasurably,
boundlessly,
limitlessly more
than all you could ever ask,
and all you could ever imagine,
all you could even conceive of
or envisage
or wildly dream of,
according to the power at work within you,
around you,
in front and behind,
dancing with you,
all-containing,
everywhere you go and everything you do,
to God be the glory!
To God be the honour, the praise,
the acclaim and the exaltation,
in the church,

the bride waiting with bated breath,
and in Christ Jesus throughout all generations,
through history,
stretching back and forth to eternity.

Amen.

Be confident in your faith, identity, hope and future as a beloved child of God, and rest in the knowledge of the truth of the gospel. Be courageous and learn contentment, even in suffering and brokenness. Be captivated and rejoice in all circumstances. Be contagious and 'shine as stars' in the world. In all this, rely on the strength of our God.

And indeed, you will run forward, arms outstretched, hands held out, catching hold of a treasure found sometimes in the darkest of places, and drawing it right into your chest, holding it close to you. As you hold it so dearly, so you will shine out with that treasure.

The caught will become the catching.

NOTES

1 Confident in our faith

1. John Ortberg, *Faith and Doubt* (Zondervan, 2008), p. 10.

2. Ibid., p. 20.

3. Gregory A. Boyd, *Is God to Blame? Beyond Pat Answers to the Problem of Suffering* (InterVarsity Press, 2003), p. 16.

2 Confident in our identity

1. From Thomas of Celano's biography of St Francis of Assisi; see <https://catholicexchange.com/st-francis-and-answering-gods-call> (accessed 22 June 2018).

2. Name changed.

3 Confident in our hope

1. Name changed.

2. Name changed.

4 Confident in our future

1. Tim Keller, *Making Sense of God: An Invitation to the Sceptical* (Hodder & Stoughton, 2016), p. 158.

2. Tom Wright, *Paul for Everyone: Philippians* (SPCK, 2010), pp. 126–127.

3. C. S. Lewis, *The Last Battle* (HarperCollins, 1956), p. 228, copyright © C. S. Lewis Pte. Ltd 1956. Extract reprinted by permission.

5 Courageous waiting

1. <www.cics.umass.edu/news/latest-news/research-online -videos> (accessed 11 June 2018).
2. <www.faithgateway.com/simeon-watching-waiting> (accessed 11 June 2018).
3. <bgbc.co.uk/wp-content/uploads/2013/11/A-Spirituality -of-Waiting-by-Henri-Nouwen.pdf> (accessed 11 June 2018).

6 Courageous brokenness

1. Catherine Campbell, *Broken Works Best* (Monarch, 2012), p. 19.
2. Ibid., p. 176.
3. Ibid., p. 176.

7 Courageous disappointment

1. Tanya Marlow, *Coming Back to God When You Feel Empty: Whispers of Restoration from the Book of Ruth* (CreateSpace Independent Publishing Platform, 2015), p. 2.
2. Ibid., p. 6.
3. Ibid., p. 8.
4. Ibid., p. 8.
5. Ibid., p. 21.
6. Ibid., p. 36.

8 Courageous perseverance

1. C. S. Lewis, *The Voyage of the Dawn Treader* (Puffin Books, 1965), p. 180, copyright © C. S. Lewis Pte. Ltd 1952. Extract reprinted by permission.
2. Name changed.

9 Captivated by worship

1. The Westminster Shorter Catechism.
2. John Piper, *Desiring God: Meditations of a Christian Hedonist* (IVP, 1986), p. 50.
3. C. S. Lewis, *Reflections on the Psalms* (Harcourt, Brace & Co., 1958), p. 97, copyright © C. S. Lewis Pte. Ltd 1958. Extract reprinted by permission.

10 Captivated by satisfaction

1. <www.bbc.co.uk/news/business-16812545> (accessed 27 September 2018).
2. Augustine's *Confessions*, Book 1, Chapter 1.
3. C. S. Lewis, *The Lion, the Witch and the Wardrobe* (Lion, 1981), p. 88, copyright © C. S. Lewis Pte. Ltd 1950. Extract reprinted by permission.

11 Captivated in darkness

1. Jean-Pierre de Caussade, *Self-Abandonment to Divine Providence* (Burns & Oates, 1959).
2. Jeremiah Burroughs, *The Rare Jewel of Christian Contentment* (Sovereign Grace, 2001), p. 5.
3. Try reading Richard Foster's *Celebration of Discipline: The Path to Spiritual Growth* (Hodder & Stoughton, 2008) for a comprehensive and helpful introduction to spiritual disciplines.

12 Captivated by surrender

1. <www.christianitytoday.com/history/people/poets/fanny-crosby.html> (accessed 11 June 2018).
2. 'Blessed Assurance' by Fanny J. Crosby (1820–1915).
3. Jeremiah Burroughs, *The Rare Jewel of Christian Contentment* (Sovereign Grace, 2001), p. 2.
4. David Hazard, *I Come Quietly to Meet You: An Intimate Journey in God's Presence* (Bethany House, 2005), p. 9.

5. These words by Amy Carmichael can be found in *Inspired Faith: 365 Days a Year* (Thomas Nelson, 2012), p. 280.
6. Hazard, *I Come Quietly*, p. 111.

14 Contagious reconciliation

1. *The Telegraph*, 8 March 2006, <www.telegraph.co.uk/news/uknews/1512403/Its-not-whether-you-can-or-cant-forgive-its-whether-you-will-or-wont.html> (accessed 12 June 2018).

15 Contagious shining stars

1. Name changed.
2. Teresa of Avila (1515–1582), <www.azquotes.com/author/19882-Teresa_of_Avila> (accessed 12 June 2018).
3. Her Majesty's Revenue and Customs.